Florida
Move
Guide

The Unofficial Moving To Florida Warning, Decision and Help Guide

Ron Stack

Disclaimer

This book is presented to provide entertainment and information only. The author and publisher are not providing any financial, tax, legal, real estate or any other professional advice or services. While reasonable effort was used in putting this book together, the author and publisher make no representations or warranties of any kind as to the accuracy or completeness of the contents. The author and publisher assume no liability of any kind with respect to the books contents. No guarantees or warranties of any kind are expressed or implied in the book or by presenting it. The author and publisher shall not be held liable or responsible to any person or entity for any loss, incidental, consequential or otherwise, any damages caused, or alleged to have been caused, directly or indirectly, by the information presented. No warranty may be created or extended by anyone who is distributing, marketing or otherwise offering this book. You should seek the services of a competent professional for any financial, tax, legal, real estate or any other advice. You will be responsible for your decisions, choices and actions.

Table of Contents

Introduction

More Than Half Move Back

Why are so many people scrambling to get out of Florida and move back home? From the year 2000 to 2009, an average of 851,262 people moved to Florida. During that same time 479,586, or more than half as many, moved out every year. It's no secret to the Florida moving companies that many who move here expecting paradise, end up paying just about any price to get out.

How could moving to Florida possibly be a mistake? Simply put, living here is a lot different than spending vacations here. On vacations you don't experience everything you will once you live here every day.

The first couple of months after I moved to Florida seemed like paradise. It was like being on a real long vacation. Within a year though, that feeling wore off. Things that never bothered me while on vacations here, started to work on me.

Before I moved, I had no idea that so many people that moved to Florida ended up moving back, or what the main reasons were. That never came up in any of the research I did. I first discovered these things while working as a Realtor in the state. Most sellers who called me, wanted to sell to get out of Florida. They said they made a huge mistake moving there. At first I didn't completely understand their frustration, but it wasn't long until I started to experience the same strong remorse myself.

Reason for Moving Back Home

The reasons given for moving back home were many but as I talked to more sellers, I realized that a few of the same reasons were mentioned by nearly everyone. Almost none of these dream killing causes were ever noticed during vacations. However, most became apparent within a surprisingly short period of time after moving here, often within the first year.

Why did I wish I knew about all this before I moved? Because selling your home to move is costly. Moving a thousand miles away is expensive. Buying another home means paying closing costs. A move like this is a big disruption to enjoying life. Can you imagine going through all that, then realizing you made a mistake and having to do it all over again?

Florida Move Mistake's High Cost

Selling up north, moving to Florida and then moving back can easily cost you $100,000 or more. The stress and misery caused can be even costlier. As their real estate agent, people have blamed the extreme stress of this mistake for divorces, bankruptcy and even heart attacks.

I am not trying to talk you out of moving to Florida. There are people who have moved here and it worked out. Why did it work for some but not for others? You will learn what causes so many folks just like you, to regret their move to Florida as well as why some say they will never leave. Hopefully this can help prevent you from making a very costly and painful mistake.

From 2000 to 2009, 851,262 people moved to Florida. 479,586 moved out. The odds of your move working out long term are not very good. This book aims to change that because you will learn before you move, what the leading issues are that cause people to move back, to help you determine if this may happen to you.

Learn How to Avoid Making a Big Mistake

You will also discover why some who moved say they will always be Floridians. Their Florida lifestyle may be a plan you never considered. I will explain this and other plans so you will know all of your options. Once you choose a plan that you think will work best for you, I will tell you how you can best be sure it will work for you. Will moving to Florida likely be the best move you ever made, or a miserable mistake? Let's find out!

Evacuations and Hurricanes

You Can't Know This Until You Live It

You have just moved to Florida after selling your comfortable home up north that you've had for years. It's been a couple of months since the move and the new place is finally starting to feel like home. The first month was hectic. It's a lot of work setting up a new home. Your family would have helped but you are too far away for that now.

It's a beautiful evening. You decide to relax while watching a TV show with your wife before going to bed. Suddenly the show is interrupted for a special emergency update. The National Hurricane Center has moved the "cone of uncertainty" over your area. Worse yet, a hurricane hunter aircraft now reports the storm offshore strengthened to a category two and further strengthening is expected. Growing into the most destructive category 5 is not impossible as the hurricane picks up strength from the warm waters just before landfall. They expect it to hit land the day after tomorrow. Mandatory evacuations are planned for your area tomorrow starting at eight o'clock in the morning. Huh?

Forced to Leave Your Home

You are told that should prepare immediately and secure your home before you leave. They again warn that this is a mandatory evacuation. If you leave too late, the winds may down trees and power lines and prevent you from getting out. They warn you that if you choose to stay, any call for help does not have to be legally responded to because doing so would put the few remaining emergency personnel at risk. That is why you must leave.

All of a sudden, it hits you. For the first time in your life, you are being ordered to leave your home. Where will you go? How long will you be gone? Will your home still be here when you return?

It's getting late. Its dark outside but it's still hot and humid. You would be attacked by swarms of mosquitoes if you went outside now and started putting up your hurricane shutters. You made sure the house you bought came with them, but you've been too busy moving that you haven't had time to figure out how to put them up. You wonder if you even have the tools needed. How heavy are those metal things anyway? It's supposed to be ninety-three degrees and humid tomorrow, how long will it take me?

You have so much to do before you pack up and leave, but it's getting late and you are both tired, and now stressed out as well. You both agree on getting a good night's sleep and starting early in the morning on what must be done. You turn in.

This news has upset your spouse so much she says she can't sleep. She says she might as well start packing. This is difficult for her. What precious items do you take and what gets left behind that you may never see again? There are far too many family pictures, heirlooms and other prized sentimental possessions to fit in a car.

No Place to Go

You decide to make reservations for a place to stay safe from the storm. After trying online and then by phone, you give up. With almost half a million people evacuating, there are no rooms left anywhere within a couple hundred miles. The travel agency promises to call if they can come up with anything.

Gas! You've heard of gas shortages happening when all those extra cars are on the road. You tell your wife you are going to fill up now. It's late, so maybe there won't be any lines, you should be right back.

As you get close to the nearest gas station you see there are already long lines formed. You call home to say it's going to take a while, you'll be home as soon as you can.

As you sit in line, you think about all the things you have to do tomorrow. Put up the hurricane shutters. Move everything from outside into the garage. Where will you put it all? You're tired and more you think about it, the more stress it causes.

The horror of living through another hurricane season with the threat of evacuations or total destruction of your home is one of the main reasons given for leaving the state. Most have never experienced this while on vacation here. It's something most prospective new Floridians never really think about. The truth is, even those who considered it couldn't imagine what it is really like to be under threat five months a year every year of losing everything you have. You have to live here and experience it. That is how most of the issues that force people to leave are. You really don't realize what it's like until you live here and are forced to go through it.

The hype of danger by the media starts around June 1st yearly. First you hear the warnings to get your "hurricane kit" together. When a hurricane goes through it can totally destroy thousands of homes, but it can also knock out power and utilities for a much larger area far away from the worst destruction. That's why you need this kit. Bottled water because you won't get it from your spigot after the storm hits. Canned food because the stores won't be open and the refrigerators won't work. Flashlights, batteries and candles because there won't be any power for light. The point is to be prepared to live without access to food, water, electric and anything you might want at a store. You must survive for weeks or months without most of life's modern conveniences.

Evacuations Ordered More Often

Evacuations can be worse because you may have to go through more than one every year. They are more likely now after Hurricane Katrina devastated New Orleans in 2005. Evacuations came late or not at all. That storm surprised emergency planners and people suffered. After TV footage showed thousands of desperate citizens trapped in the Superdome without adequate food, water and restroom facilities for a long period of time, the authorities now error on the side of caution. You are now less likely to be in an area that a hurricane hits, but you are also much more likely to be told you must evacuate and leave your home.

I've seen the aftermath of a hurricane up close with my own eyes. You can be trapped in a home with no air conditioning in the Florida summer heat and humidity. The streets will be littered with downed trees and telephone poles, electrical wires and roofs that make using your car or truck impossible.

For thousands of former residents their dream of moving to Florida to relax and enjoy the warm weather ended with losing their home and all their personal possessions. After Hurricane Charley landed in Florida as the first of the record setting 2004 season, I ventured out after a few weeks to see the damage. Seeing the devastation with your own eyes, standing on the ground is totally different than a two minute piece on the 6 o'clock news. It looked like a war zone that had been nuked. There were large areas where the homes didn't have roofs anymore. It was like a giant weed whacker went through and cut all the homes, power lines and trees in half. Furniture, family photos, kids toys were mixed in with the debris among downed tree and power lines.

One of the main complaints from those that decided to leave the state was the stress they went through every time storm is named. Watching constant emergency updates and worrying until the storm makes land fall or is no longer a threat takes its toll. Most hurricanes move at the rate of 10-15 mph and are tracked from the time they are just a tropical storm far out in the

Gulf or Atlantic Ocean. This is well before the authorities can determine where it is likely to go. You will hear about it on the news constantly and if your area falls within the 5 day cone of uncertainty, you have to decide when to do your hurricane prep drill.

This consists of checking your hurricane kit to make sure you have enough food, the batteries are still good, and you have plenty of bottled water and other supplies. You have to decide when to bring all of your outside stuff into the house or the garage. If you don't, your chaise lounges, table and chairs, grill, lawn ornaments and anything else will get blown away or could become a lethal projectile if picked up by 120+ mph winds.

Preparing Your Home Before You Evacuate

The tricky part about this is the timing. You don't want to bring the stuff in too early because if the cone of danger moves away from your area you wasted your time. Keep in mind this will not be pleasant. This happens in the 6 months of a Florida summer, it is hot and humid. You also don't want to wait too long because moving that stuff when the hurricane is too close can be impossible with wind gusts strong enough to blow you around and frequent violent thunderstorms.

You may have to do this many times during a single hurricane season. The storms are given names starting with the letter "A" for the first one every year. In 2005 the last hurricane to hit the state was named Wilma.

The next issue you must decide on during this prep time is your hurricane shutters. Most new homes in the lower to middle price ranges are sold with metal hurricane shutters. They are usually stacked together neatly in the garage and bolted to a wall. You are to take these and put them up around all the openings of your home such as windows and doors. Again, it's all about timing. You have to be extra careful about this because although they are not light, if you try to put them up in strong winds could get blown away. If you thought about hiring someone to do it for you, good luck. Thousands of others have that same idea and getting someone is next to impossible.

You could put them up early, but once you do your home will become like a cave. No light gets in. When all the shutters are up, you can't tell if its midnight or sunny outside. It's just dark inside your home in the Sunshine State.

That's why some people put them up and take them down for every threat regardless of the hassle, heat and humidity. A growing number are getting tired of that, and putting them up when the first threat comes and leaving them up for the whole season. They choose to live in the dark over constantly putting them up and taking them down in the Florida summer heat.

There are other options like clear shutters and shatter proof windows. They are costly but offer more convenience. They do have drawbacks. That will be covered in a latter chapter.

While you are coordinating the shutters and the outside stuff, you also have to be ready to implement your evacuation plan. Fill the gas tank early because the pumps can go dry when hundreds of thousands of people are ordered to leave their home and make an unplanned trip. You don't want to run out of gas on the interstate in a hurricane traffic jam.

What Doesn't Fit in the Car, Lost Forever?

When ordered to leave your home, you have to decide what possessions you cherish most. You have to remember that there is a possibility that anything you leave behind could be lost forever. I always kept a list of what I was going to take, and where they were located. It was a lot easier that way because I didn't have think about it, I just packed.

Waiting until an evacuation is ordered to travel makes it more difficult. You will have the company of thousands, possibly hundreds of thousands of people that must do the same thing. It may be impossible to get reservations for any place to stay anywhere within a day's drive. During the summer, tourist can already have most hotels well booked up.

I had a couple of hotels in center of the state picked out to evacuate to because they had very good cancellation policies. I made reservations whenever there was even a possibility a hurricane might threaten my area. I would cancel without a charge if they weren't needed. Having the hotel picked out, phone numbers and travel directions handy meant I had less to think about when an emergency approached.

Another complaint of waiting until an evacuation is ordered is the travel. The roads taking you out of harm's way become a traffic nightmare. Expect ten mph stop and go bumper to bumper traffic that causes lots of fender benders and accidents to make things worse. Since this involves so many more cars on the road than usual, gas stations run out of gas. People also have hoarded gas for their home generators to power their home since there will often be power outages after the storm.

You may be stuck idling in stopped traffic on the interstate with your gauge on empty. You may be lucky enough to get off at the next exit before you run out of gas only to find the gas stations have no gas left. Cars out of gas clog the roads. Fender benders and exhausted, stressed out people on the side of the road in the heat humidity and rain, it's not a place I wish for you to be.

If you leave before the order, you can avoid this. I often did this to avoid any possibility of being a part of that mess. If the hurricane changed course and there wasn't an evacuation, I just looked at it like a short vacation. I didn't miss much during those few days because not many people want to look at real estate with a hurricane heading that way.

Some have told me they leave late, after everybody

else and the roads clear. I would not suggest this because when a major hurricane is even a hundred miles away you will have blinding rain and wind gusts that will blow your car around. Driving at interstate speed and not being able to see anything because of the amount of rain pounding the windshield is not fun.

If you need to work to support a family, consider what the effect hurricane season could have on your income. Preparing for, and evacuating can be disruptive to your paycheck. On top of that, you have the extra cost of gas, accommodations and meals out. If you are on a fixed retirement income or work to support a young growing family and living paycheck to paycheck, an evacuation could cause a financial crisis. If a storm destroys your place of employment, it could be a long term one.

You could move to Florida and avoid some of this. Coastal areas are much more likely to be affected by storms than those farther inland. Most prospective new residents want to move near the coast. If you moved to certain areas in the middle of the state, the chance of ever having to go through a mandatory evacuation or direct hit can be very small. Hurricanes lose power when they interact with land.

Is This What You Signed Up For

If you are retiring and looking for a place to relax, do you really want to move somewhere that you will have to worry about "hurricane season" five months every year? Do you want to see your wife or husband try to decide what sentimental things to pack into the car and what to leave behind that could be lost forever? How will you feel when told you must leave your home for your own safety? Are you prepared to intentionally put yourself and your family in a home that you could be repeatedly forced to leave, or have it totally destroyed?

Fun Hurricane Facts

Every second, a major hurricane unleashes energy equivalent to multiple atomic bombs.

In 1999 Hurricane Floyd just a category 1 on the 1-5 hurricane scale, destroyed 19 million trees while causing $1,000,000,000 in damage.

Jupiter a planet much larger than the earth has a hurricane the size of earth which has been going on for over 300 years.

"Interesting Hurricane Facts" April 11, 2011 6:41:15 PM. April 11, 2011. http://www.hurricane-facts.com/Interesting-Hurricane-Facts.php

Missing Family Friends Home

Holidays without Family and Friends

Most of the people I met in Florida moved from an area that they lived most of their lives. They learned to drive, went on their first date and got their first job there. There where many positive memories were made. They often loved the area, but didn't realize it until they moved away from it.

I met a nice couple we'll call Bob and Mary when they moved from Michigan and bought a home from me here in Florida. They had lived in the same area outside of Detroit all of their lives. They dreamed of moving to Florida for years. They vacationed here many times. They thought moving to escape the cold Michigan winters was a great idea. So when Bob retired from the plant, they made the decision to move.

Bob and Mary put their home in Michigan up for sale. They had lived in the home for over two decades. They raised their three children there, but they were now all out on their own. Two of them had children of their own.

There were a lot of wonderful family memories attached to that home. They told me that every year at Thanksgiving, Christmas and other holidays; all of the kids and grandchildren would gather and spend most of the day at their home. It was like "home base".

The home they bought in Florida was not far from where they spent many vacations. Their new home was less than 10 minutes to the beach, had a pool and

Hopewell School

From the desk of Miss Carter...

Jim
860 -
490.0259

there were dozens of golf courses within a short drive. Everything seemed perfect. It was working out just like they planned and they were happy those first few months.

As the first set of holidays since the move approached, Mary decided it might be a good time to start making plans for Thanksgiving. Everybody always came to their home for the holiday, and she was hoping that would continue. Mary loved preparing a big family meal and seeing everybody together.

They now lived over 1000 miles away from the kids and grand kids, so new arrangements would have to be made. Mary made calls "back home" to invite everybody down to their new home for Thanksgiving.

The kids were not as enthusiastic as she had hoped. They would have to take time off from work. The kids had school. Everybody promised they would discuss it and let her know.

Over the next couple of weeks Mary learned that because of work, school and other commitments, only one family could make it. She was a little upset. Although she talked to the kids and grand kids every week, she hadn't seen them since the move and she really missed them. She was looking forward to seeing her son, his wife and the two little ones even if it will only be for a couple of days.

Mary had been experiencing mixed emotions about the move, but didn't say anything to Bob. They had met some of the neighbors, but said they didn't really connect with any of them. She was lonely and really looking forward to Thanksgiving.

The week before the holiday, her son called and told her the grand-kids had gotten the flu, so they weren't able to make it. Bob told me Mary wasn't the same after that. When Bob and Mary sat down to a Thanksgiving meal by themselves, Mary began to cry. That's the first time she told Bob that she thought moving may have been a mistake, and she wanted to move back.

New Doctor, Dentist, Hair Stylist, Everything

This happens a lot. It is a major reason people leave Florida and move back. Sometimes it happens quickly, sometimes it takes years. It can be hard to know the impact on your life of being so far away from all of your family and friends, until you actually experience it. With all of the research and planning people do, they never really consider how different living so far from the rest of the family would be.

Sometimes You Don't Know What You Have Until

Chances are you have lived in your current home for many years. You may have bought, sold and called a couple of other houses "home" before you moved into your current one. Moving from to a larger, more comfortable, better located home in the same general area was a great experience. Your family was still close. You still worked at the same job. You were still close enough to get together with friends you've had for a long time. When you move to a better home in the same area, the home changes but everything else stays the same.

That's not true when you move a thousand miles away. Where you buy groceries, your dentist, doctor all change. How will you handle not having any family members nearby for support? Do you really want to start all over and try to find new friends? A move like this this means you must find a new doctor and dentist that you feel comfortable with. Trust me, this can be a real challenge in Florida. Who will cut your hair? I never looked the same after moving to Florida because no one could cut my hair anything like the one up north could. Will you find a place of worship that you like? If you have children, how traumatic will starting a new school with different systems be for them? Even if you spent many one week vacations in this new area, you probably don't have any idea what attorney you would call if you needed one, for example.

More Time More Courses, But Lost Desire

I once got a call from a man who wanted to sell his home in Florida after less than a year of moving there because he couldn't find any good golf buddies. Golf was a favorite thing in his life. After he retired, he convinced his reluctant wife to sell a home they lived in for 35 years in New York and move to Florida.

The area they moved to was like heaven for golf fanatics. It had a lot more courses than up north and you can play all year long. They bought a place right on the fairway of a great course.

This guy joined a few organizations and volunteered at a couple of others to meet other golfers he might enjoy playing a round with. After a while, he realized he just didn't click with any of the new people the way he did with his long time golf buddies up north. They didn't have the same sense of humor. They couldn't be counted on to show up regularly. The members of the group changed constantly and sometimes no one showed up at all. After almost a year he realized that one of the things he enjoyed about golf so much was socializing with great group of friends.

This guy now lived on a beautiful lush golf course surrounded by many more. The weather allowed play all year long. He lived in a golfer's paradise but he no longer enjoyed the game. His wife never really wanted to move in the first place. She missed the grand kids. They decided they were moving back home.

If Family or Friends Move Down

If you are moving to Florida to be near family or friends, your chances of satisfaction with your move will be much higher than most. I worked with couple who bought a home to move to when they retire. Retirement was still a few years off. They came down for vacations in the meantime and often brought family and friends with them. It was a three bedroom home, 10 minutes from a beautiful beach and the warm Gulf of Mexico waters. Over the next few years, three other families that were friends of theirs also bought future retirement homes all on the same street as the first couple. When they all move here full time they will be surrounded with the same network of longtime friends.

Another successful move to a more tropical climate started with a job transfer. This Young couple called on a home for sale ad I was running. They were married with 1 small child. The husband was transferred from Illinois to the area I sold in. I found them a home in a nice, quiet, safe area with good public schools. Shortly after they closed on the home and moved in they called to tell me that the wife's parents were in town, staying with them and they were interested in looking at homes for themselves.

While showing homes to the parents, I learned that their daughter that moved here was an only child. So when she moved away they immediately started to miss their only daughter and grandchild. They bought a place near their daughter and moved down. Over the next couple of years I was contacted to help find homes for different members of the husband's family. Whenever I run into them at a restaurant or store they always seem to be with some of their extended family. They have told me how glad they were to have made the move. Living near other family is one of the main reasons why.

I am not suggesting that the only way a move to Florida will work for you is if all your friends and family move with you. I am suggesting that you should give serious thought as to how much a part of your life your friends and family are, before you move. Do you do things together often? Do you have a weekly card night or golf day? Do you have frequent dinner parties, barbeques, or other reasons you regularly get together? During football season do you get together with a group of friends to watch the game? A thoughtful assessment of what you will be giving up could save you a lot of money, time and heartache.

There are people of course who move down and don't miss anybody or anything from back home. If you are not a part of a large family, or you dread the couple of times a year you do see them, a long distance move may be perfect for you. If the only time you see the relatives is on Christmas day and a big fight always breaks out, you may not miss that. If you don't have family close to you and the only close friends you have just got divorced, moving far away might not leave you feeling lonely. After giving it some serious thought, if you decide a long distance move is worth pursuing there are ways to test it. We will talk about that in a latter chapter.

A Grandfathers Love By Sara Teasdale

They said he sent his love to me,

They wouldn't put it in my hand,

And when I asked them where it was,

They said I couldn't understand.

I though they must have hidden it,

I hunted for it all the day,

And when I told them so at night,

They smiled at turned their heads away.

They say that love is something kind,

That I can never see or touch.

I wish he'd sent me something else,

I like his cough drops twice as much.

You Can't Escape This

Longer Hotter More Humid Summers

I have talked to thousands of prospective new
Floridians and the warm weather is a main reason
they want to move here, or it's in the top three. Tired
of the cold winters, they want to move to Florida and
nail their old snow shovel to a tree in the front yard.
The funny thing is heat and humidity is in the top
three reasons given by people who want to move out.

I make living selling homes. So after spending a
fortune on advertising I don't try to talk buyers that
call on the phone out of buying a home here. I'm great
at sales but if I tried to warn buyers about the heat and
humidity when they call on a home, they would think
I'm nuts. Even my own relatives that visit think I'm
crazy when I complain about the heat. While visiting
in June they tell me it's not that bad. Of course, they
are at the beach and in my pool cooling off all day.
They look lobster-like red after only a week. You can't
do that every day of the year if you live here, unless
you want the skin of a ninety year old when you're
only thirty five.

Thousands of families leave Florida every year
blaming the six to nine months of heat and humidity
as one of the main reasons. Even if these same people
were warned about it ahead of time, they still would
have moved here because they don't believe it's a big
deal? Why?

One reason is most people have vacationed here
during the summer for a week, and survived. Even if

you stood in long lines at Disney for an hour to get on a ride, it didn't seem so bad because you were distracted from the heat by the newness and excitement of the park. That's vacation. Now go to that same park every day for 30 days straight in summer and see if you notice any changes. I'd be willing to bet that every day you would be a little less thrilled by the rides and a lot more aware of the brutal heat, humidity, and the long lines. That's living here.

Another reason prospective new residents to the "swamp" state dismiss the heat caution is because they will tell you that they have the same thing back home. That's not quite accurate. Back home, summer only lasts three months, and has cooler weather right before, and right after it. The sun is stronger and will burn you faster. Florida's summer is six to nine months long. You don't have that back home.

I've experienced years where it seemed like the humidity lasted the entire year. Florida is much closer to the equator than "back home". The sun is much stronger during the traditional summer months and as it is all year long. As a resident, you learn to avoid any direct exposure to it except maybe during the winter. Failure to do so will quickly insure premature aging of the skin, possibly worse. That is why dermatologist and those that cut cancer from the skin do a brisk business in Florida.

A family formerly from Ohio who wanted to move back called me to list their home. They complained about the weather among other things. "In Ohio it gets hot, it gets humid, but not for 9 months straight without a break" he told me.

The hot days with high humidity in the north that happen only occasionally can't prepare you for the long summers in Florida. Ninety plus degree days with high humidity week after week, starts to takes its toll after four, five months or longer. That's why there are always lots of moving vans loaded with prized possessions heading north on I-95 and I-75.

It's like being told for the first time not to touch the stove because it's hot. You may or may not believe it, but if you do touch it, you will know it forever. That's what living with the heat in Florida is like. If you are thinking living here full time, please read about how to test that idea first, later in the book.

Recess is supposed to be Fun

Shortly after I sold a home to a young family new to the state, I saw their name in the newspaper. Their son had a heat stroke while at school on lunch recess. It was only the beginning of May but it already felt like the middle of summer by up north standards. I called them and was told that he was fine, but it was very scary. They said nothing like that had ever happened to him before. They were surprised by the incident and now more concerned about the heat. They were afraid it could happen again but not end with the same positive outcome.

The newspaper took the incident as opportunity to caution and inform. Turns out heat stroke is very common down here and happens to people of all ages. Many seemingly normal activities can put you in danger here, where back north you never had to think about it. People die from this every year. Seniors in their middle sixties and older must be especially careful because their bodies can't adjust to temperature easily, and they may be on medication that can make it even harder for the body to regulate temperature. You may want to check with your doctor about medications you taking before considering a move to a hotter climate.

A Different Golf Stroke

For most of the US, summer is prime time for golf and most courses are closed in the winter. Not so in Florida. Winter is prime time and that is when you will be charged the highest rates. Most courses cut their rates dramatically in April or May. From May through September you can expect to pay half price or less depending upon the day. Heat and humidity are the reason.

Summer discounts get larger as the sun gets stronger and the heat index rises. You can play almost anywhere after two in the afternoon, for half or less than the regular rate. You can get 18 holes in easily because nobody else will be out there to hold you up and it stays light until 9:30 p.m.

I've had many different golf buddies in Florida through the years, but none that played consistently. A contractor Friend of mine loved golf but stopped playing because it got too crowded in the winter and he couldn't take the heat in the summer.

Another friend in real estate first got into golf in his fifties and loved it. The only thing he loved more than golf was saving money. He always complained about the humidity but still would only play after two in the afternoon to get the lowest possible price. One outing around the 12th hole I noticed he wasn't saying much. He looked pale. He said he didn't feel well but wanted to continue. When we got out of the cart to hit his next shot he stumbled and fell. I helped him into the cart and rushed him back to the clubhouse. I was afraid he was having a heart-attack. He got the attention he needed. It wasn't a heart-attack, it was a heat stroke. He never played again.

The Sun on Steroids

Many a new Floridian have given in to the temptation to trade their trusty up north car or truck, for a convertible. If you too have thought of this, you may want to reconsider. Between spring and fall up north, you'll probably have more days to enjoy a ride with the top down than you will in Florida all year. Winter in Florida is convertible weather. Most of the rest of the year it is too hot and humid to enjoy, there are occasional swarms of various bugs and violent thunder showers roll in quickly. The biggest worry is probably the sun.

Most weather reports will report the UV index, especially during the six months of summer. It tells you how long you can be exposed to the sun before your skin begins to burn. Many days it is less than five minutes. I've met many long term Floridians whose face was like leather from working outside or driving their convertible. The sun is much stronger here. If you want your skin to look 10-30 years older than you are or have skin cancer cut off your face, don't show the Florida sun the respect it deserves.

Sauna Scenarios

I know many Floridian wannabes never consider humidity before moving south. Nothing about living up north prepares you for living in a humid summer six to nine months or more a year, every year. For most folks, the longer you're here the more it aggravates you.

This is precisely like many of the other reasons that cause people to decide to move back. First, even when warned about it ahead of time, you don't believe it will affect you. Secondly, when experienced only in short periods like when on a one week vacation or a shorter northern summer it isn't such a big deal. It has a cumulative effect. If you ever enjoyed taking in a sauna, a little time spent in the steam followed by a shower is refreshing. If you did that many times a day for six months, you would probably find it anything but refreshing anymore.

Humidity was mentioned to me repeatedly as one of the major factors in selling to move back home. In a latter chapter there will be helpful suggestions that will help you decide whether this will be a big factor for you or not. Until then, here's a list of scenarios you may want to picture yourself in. You may say that happens to you now during summer. That may be true, but you have a weaker summer for three months a year. Now multiply it by two or three.

When you walk out the door the humidity smacks you in the face, makes you instantly feel sweaty and uncomfortable, like you need to shower.

Your sunglasses fog up from humidity when going from inside to outside your home, car or store.

After being in a store for only a few minutes, you return to your car to find it is already 160 degrees inside. Do you stand outside in 95 degree 95% humidity and wait for the A/C to cool the car down or do you get in, stick to the seat and tolerate the 150 degree heat.

You park your car in the garage (everybody here that has one has an auto garage door opener). An half an hour latter you go into the garage that is now 120 degrees because of the heat from the car's engine. Sweat some more.

You spent a fortune on outdoor furniture to eat and relax outside and enjoy the Florida lifestyle like the people in the brochure. In reality it's too hot and humid to comfortably enjoy a meal outdoors most of the year, unless you like the extra salty taste you get from sweat dripping into your food.

You paid a lot of extra money for a pool, only to learn that 90 degree pool water doesn't offer any relief from 95 degree humid days.

Heat Stroke Facts

Heat stroke symptoms: headache, muscle cramps, fatigue, dizziness, hot dry skin, flushed skin, high body temperature, unable to sweat, rapid pulse, rapid breathing, disorientation, seizures, loss of consciousness

Heat stroke complications: unconsciousness, shock, coma, permanent brain damage, death

"Complications of Heatstroke". Wednesday, January 26, 2011 8:13:00AM. April 11, 2011.
http://www.wrongdiagnosis.com/h/heatstroke/complic.htm

43

Ride the Money Roller Coaster

The Economy is Worse or Better More Often

Money problems, mainly not having enough of it was another common theme cited for needing to move back north. Some people would just come out and tell me everything even though I didn't ask. Others would blame other things but you could tell that they were experiencing financial stress. The fickle see-saw economy of Florida can negatively affect retirees on a fixed budget as well as those who still need to work for income. Changes in the economy, increasing taxes, fast rising insurance rates and other financial matters that seem to happen overnight, were singled out the most.

The cost of living in the state of Florida had been much lower than most other states for decades. You could move from just about anywhere else in the US to Florida and buy a home comparable to the one you left for a lot less money. Taxes were lower. Insurance was reasonable. The wages were lower so the cost of goods and services was lower. That's one reason so many people moved to the state when they retired. Their money, social security and pensions could buy them a very comfortable retirement, often better than where they had moved from.

That started to change in the early 2000's Real estate values started to climb. Higher value led to higher taxes. The state that promised retirees warm weather and a stable low cost of living was changing.

The state's economy now seems to be in permanent roller coaster mode, and that presents a problem that you need to consider. Florida' booms are hotter and its recessions can be deeper than what you are now used to. This presents a planning challenge especially to those on a fixed income such as retirees and those with lower incomes like a young couple working to support a growing family. If you are looking at moving down when economy is in recession, home prices, rents and taxes may be very low. If you base your decision on these lower numbers because you can afford it now that will probably turn out to be a mistake. In the not too distant future, the economy will heat up again and rising real estate taxes rent and other costs may cause you financial distress.

I've had to sell homes for many on a fixed income because the cost of living in Florida had risen far faster that their retirement income. Often they've had to move back home and move in with family. Or they tell me that homes in the state they came from are now more affordable than Florida. Financial problems plus the other reasons mentioned earlier caused these people to leave the state.

Young people often sell a home up north, come away from closing with a nice little nest egg and buy a home here. Anyway, after not finding employment or working for lower wages than they expected, they would want to sell and move back. The combination of financial struggle, heat and lack of family support causes them to need to move back.

Scrambled Nest Egg

When this happens and you need to sell fast, you often end up getting far less for your home than you would like. If you bought during a boom and now selling into a common Florida bust, you will leave your nest egg here. I've seen it happen a lot. Some who became victims of a bad Florida economy have had to borrow money just to get out of the state.

Rarely did retired Floridians given employment as a reason for deciding to leave the state. Many do work to get out of the house for a couple of hours or earn a few extra bucks. I have noticed an increase of seniors who say they must now work to make ends meet.

If you are flexible on hours, wages and benefits, you may find work, particularly part time. Pay in Florida in usually low when compared to most other states. Some blame retirees who will work for any amount, for the low wages. Restaurants need cooks and waitresses, grocery stores need cashiers and baggers. Yes baggers. In a state with a higher percentage of senior citizens than most, many grocery stores have baggers who will also insist on pushing the cart to your car and place the bags in your car for you.

Full time employment with health benefits and a higher wage that can support a growing young family can be hard to come by. Health care of course is an exception because of the large percentage of older citizens. If you work in this field, you can be hired quickly with higher pay even before you move to the state.

48

Construction is another area that can provide high wages and plenty of work, but that depends where in the boom and bust real estate market you are. If a hurricane has caused hundreds of millions of dollars in damages to an area, you can find work at good pay because all that damage has to be repaired or replaced. Since there will be insurance dollars to pay for it, that will lift an area's economy like a giant bubble. Then the bubble will burst and you will be let go.

If you are moving to an area that is experiencing explosive growth because of retirees flocking to the place, you can get hired just by showing up. I have seen new construction so hot that contractors would drive around and try to hire people right off other contractor's job sites.

If you were looking for work in construction after a bust, forget it. In Florida, the booms are hotter and the busts are the worst you'll find anywhere. When it's hot, everybody is getting rich. When it all stops, builders who were supposed to warrant repairs on your new home go broke and leave town. The pawn shops fill with tools of the construction trades. Have you ever been on a roller coaster?

Starting or Buying a Business

It didn't take me long to notice something quite different about Florida compared to the state I came from. When selling real estate, buyers have to give you basic income and asset information so you determine what they can afford. Overall, the wages that workers earned in Florida was lower than in other states. The owners of small businesses however, made more than they probably would in another state.

During boom times, new residents pour into the state. This can happen very quickly. I watched the population explode in my area and not a single new business opened for a while. This meant long lines at restaurants to sit down for a meal or being 10 cars back at the drive through. Want a new home built? Can you wait a year or a year and a half? Fast growth provided lots of extra cash for the small business owners. More customers must spend their money with you because there were no new competitors.

Beware though, because the boom times are usually quickly followed by a bust. I had a customer who was a general contractor. After a hurricane came through a nearby area, his business took off. He signed millions in contracts to repair the damage. More workers had to be brought in from other states to handle all the work.

Unemployment was unheard of. Builders were throwing up new homes like crazy. Because these new workers were working 7 days a week and making lot of cash, the stores and restaurants were filled.

Buyers would walk into a model home, but if the builder didn't have something they could move into right away, the buyer would walk right out. That's why builders started to put up spec homes all over the place. They would borrow a bunch of money and put up a bunch of homes so when people demanded a new home right now, the builder would have one to sell them.

I got a call from an old customer, a contractor about a worker of his who wanted to buy a new home. This young kid had moved to Florida from Michigan with his girlfriend. He was working 7 days a week and had saved enough money to buy a home. They bought a brand new three bedroom, two bath, two car garage home through me for $214,000 near the height of a boom that lasted for about 2 ½ years. After the millions in insurance for hurricane rebuilding ran out, the contractors started laying workers off. This young guy was let go.

Real estate values started to sink. This was simple supply and demand. All the newly unemployed families had to sell and move, but nobody was buying. Everybody was selling. The young guy from Michigan didn't even try to sell, because the value dropped so fast. He owed far more than the home was now worth. At one point his home was decreasing in value about $5000 a month. After he moved back to Michigan, his foreclosed home came on the market for $115,000, $100,000 less than it was bought for just 2 years prior. After working mostly seven days a week for years, this guy and what became his small family, left the state with nothing.

Florida was one of the states that the housing bust started in and has been hit the hardest. It hit hard in my area because there were very few employers other than construction and tourism related businesses. Both came to an abrupt halt.

When the building stopped, thousands of workers became unemployed. These unemployed workers stopped spending money. Restaurants, tire stores and real estate agencies started to fail and close. My favorite wine and beer shop closed. I knew they were in trouble when one trip there, they shut down the coolers and only sold room temp spirits.

The builders now had thousands of finished homes and more under construction, but no buyers. All of a sudden, the buyers disappeared. I could sit at an open house in a brand new model home for 7 days a week and not have anyone stop or call on the phone for weeks at a time.

Banks started to foreclose on these unsold new homes. Many homeowners lost a lot of money. Buyers who came down and paid $250,000 cash for a home, now had a home worth maybe half that, if you could find a buyer at all. Buyers who put a lot of money down and got a mortgage to buy, saw that equity disappear as the value dropped below what they owed. For a lot of those folks, that was their whole nest egg.

A customer of mine who was a contractor didn't fare any better. After working hard for years and putting lots of money out for labor and materials on hundreds of new spec homes, the builders he contacted with couldn't sell those homes and went bust. They owed him hundreds of thousands of dollars, but couldn't pay. His business closed. He was forced to get a job far from his home and commuted home to his wife and family on weekends. He spends the little free time he has to file lawsuits and liens to try to get paid for the work he did, but often there's nothing left to go after. Beware of the Florida boom and bust cycles.

Moving to Florida and starting a new business may be a great income idea and provide a much needed service to the community. You just need to look at the area closely, and most importantly, find out where in the boom and bust cycle that area is in at the moment. That isn't as hard to do as it sounds. You can start right from where you live now. Pick an area and call five real estate agents. If only one gets back to you, times are good. If you call five and speak to all of them right away could be a lean period.

Big Money in Grab Bars Business

These days, finding a need and filling it can put a lot of cash in your pocket. That means serving seniors in most of Florida. I worked with a couple that was looking for a luxurious pool home on water with access to the Gulf of Mexico. They loved to fish, and the home they were looking for, had to have a dock in the back for the new boat they just bought. They were doing very well.

They were willing to pay cash and were looking for a good deal. They had their own small business for years. What did they do? Grab bars. Just grab bars and nothing else. Having a grab bar in the shower and other areas for safety and convenience was apparently something many seniors desired. They were the grab bar kings for all the surrounding counties. They had a small crew that installed lots of them every day. I had no idea there was so much money in something like that.

A word of caution, in the past there were fly by night operators that took advantage of senior citizens. They sold home sites where you couldn't build a home. They did shoddy home repair work. To prevent this from happening today, State licenses and permits are usually required for almost everything and they aren't easy to get. Just because you ran a roofing company up north, doesn't necessarily mean you can just start one in Florida. You will probably have to do a lot more to start doing business in Florida, including becoming certified by the state. Certified experience, notarized statements, bonding, workman's comp and more may be needed. This could have something to do with the lack of competing businesses and higher profits for small business owners. Investigate any plan thoroughly before investing.

Interesting Economic Facts

Florida's per person income growth rate dropped to 45th in the US in 2009.

More Floridians are living in poverty in 2009 than 2008 and more than 10% of residents lived on food stamps.

The rate of growth of the total value of Florida's goods and services slowed from 2006 to 2009 making the state rank 47th in the US.

Population growth is what has fueled Florida's economy in the past. That growth has slowed to near zero, and some projections show it won't return to its historic growth for at least 20 years.

"Troubling Trends Threaten Florida's Well Being". Florida Center For Fiscal And Economic Policy. Annual Economic Review July 2009. PDF file at: http://www.aboutpinellaskids.org/economicreviewtroublingtren dsthreatflorida.pdf

Environmental Downgrading

The Beaches and Fishing

Probably one of the reasons you are considering Florida is its natural beauty. Its tropical climate produces lush scenery including the famous palm tree. You can easily grow oranges and grapefruit in your back yard. The place is filled with many variations of birds and other wildlife. What you may not know from vacations here is the full effect growth and other factors have had on this beauty. No, I am not a tree hugging environmentalist, but no long time Floridian can ignore the changes that have taken place, often for the worse.

The first few years I lived in Florida I loved the beach. I was on the west coast and lived about 6 minutes from a quiet little beach village on a narrow key. The beach was very clean, not crowded and the water was warm and clear most of the year. It was just like in the travel brochures. Postcard perfect. Then things started to change.

First the road expansion started. The sleepy two lane main road was expanded to four to six lanes with a higher speed limit. At first this did not bother me at all. I was in the business of selling homes. More lanes, more people. More people meant more homes would be built, which meant more sales and money. I did not realize it at the beginning but the environment paid a price for this growth.

The larger road brought more traffic and people almost immediately. The sleepy subdivisions were soon noisy little boom areas with trucks of all types flying around as ground everywhere was being torn up to build homes.

The small peaceful beach village started to change too. The "old Florida" mom and pop businesses were being bought and torn down to make way for new high rise buildings on the beach. Cozy 10 unit old Florida beach motels with character were replaced by sixty units of cold concrete. That often meant a large loss of natural Florida vegetation that surrounded the quaint old Florida building, replaced by macadam parking lots. Hundreds of palm trees destroyed a few token ones to take their place.

More Macadam

Because there were now more people, the beach parking lots began to fill up. If you drove to the beach you were not guaranteed to be able to see it because there may not be a place for you to park. Of course they solved this problem by expanding the parking lots. Because the old lots were surrounded by road and condos, they expanded the macadam towards the water. This meant more parking but less beach. To pay for this, formerly free or low cost parking now isn't. Before, you could pay one low fee for the entire day. You now pay by the hour. You now pay more to go to less beach. More people on less sand means more litter and cigarettes in the sand and floating in the water. Welcome to the new improved paradise.

When you come to Florida to shop for a home, you may be driving up and down subdivisions of homes with picture perfect lawns. Lush green grass, beautiful perfectly trimmed bushes, and not a weed in site. If you go to a condo complex or visit a golf course, everything looks so neat and manicured. No weeds and no bugs, both of which the real Florida are loaded with. What happened to all the weeds and bugs?

More Beach Closings

Navigating your car down a quiet residential street in the morning here provides a clue. You will see a small army of trucks and trailers parked all over the road. Most won't have their four-ways on or give you any kind of warning they are parked. They are the workers who cut the grass, spray the lawns for weeds and apply fertilizer. Others will be spraying pesticides for bugs. Picture perfect weed less bug-less lawns don't just happen on their own. They get that way by constantly applying massive amounts of toxic chemicals. The problem is the rain washes all that all that pesticide, weed killer, and fertilizer into the very water that washes up onto the beaches that everybody loves so much.

What is Red Tide

For the first five years I lived in Florida during the nineties, I enjoyed the local beaches without interruption. Then the first episode of red tide happened. The scientist still don't know everything about this toxic algae bloom, but they believe it feeds off of the fertilizer and other runoff that gets washed into the water. Once the chemicals are washed into the warm water and heated by the strong Florida sun, the bloom explodes.

What the authorities do know is the bloom takes all of the oxygen out of the water and kills all the fish, crabs, and whatever else that used to live in the water. The first time it happened, I went to the beach to see for myself. What I saw was sickening.

Dead rotting fish rolling in the surf, rotting carcasses all along the beaches, as far as I could see in both directions. The smell made me want to vomit. This algae releases toxins into the air, and the wind can carry it inland for miles, causing respiratory problems in some people. I started to gag from the smell and had to leave. I did not go fishing or eat local seafood in a restaurant since that sight. Years later, I still remember that vividly.

That was not the only outbreak. It became common. It happened more often some years and never happened others. The problem is the experts believe that the fertilizer used on lawns and in agriculture of which Florida is a leader, makes the problem worse. If that's true, as more people move here it will continue to get worse.

There was a Canadian couple who rented a beautiful pool home across the street from me every winter. He was a lawyer with a successful practice that allowed him and his wife to come down every February for a month to escape the cold Canadian winter. They had been doing this for over a decade.

One year we had a red tide outbreak that was

particularly bad. It started in the summer and lasted into the winter in varying strengths. This Canadian couple looked forward to going to the beach to soak up some warm rays, go for a swim, and do a little fishing. If they didn't catch anything, they had a favorite little beachfront restaurant they would visit. They usually went to the beach almost every day when they were here, but red tide changed all that. The wife got sick the first day they were there from the smell. Red tide was present for the entire month they were there. This prevented them from enjoying the very thing they liked most, the beach. They were so disgusted after traveling that far to get here, they swore they would never come back. I never saw them again.

As a businessman in Florida, I first welcomed the growth spurts. More development means more money. But the more they ripped up old Florida to replace it with more macadam and larger taller concrete buildings, the more I sensed a loss. Quaint historic buildings with character were being replaced with massive parking lots and malls holding the same old chain stores you can find in Cleveland or Detroit.

I never thought I would be against growth or development, but living here for so many years and watching areas that give Florida's a unique charm being destroyed makes you think. They give us more man made blandness, less natural beauty. More pesticides, weed killer, oil and fecal matter washing into the once pristine waters and less fish, pelicans and dolphins. Left unchecked, the very things that attract people to the state will be destroyed. Then people won't come here anymore. Maybe that's what is already happening.

Water Fire and Crawlers

Drought and Drinking Water

Over the last several years the weather pattern here like most of the country seems to be changing. Florida has a rainy season that begins in June and ends in September. During the summer, you could count on the days being mostly sunny but at some point every day the sky would turn black and you would get a downpour. This would usually happen late in the afternoon and last for about a half hour. Then the sun would come back out, dry things up quickly and you would go about your day. It doesn't always happen like that anymore.

In recent times Florida has suffered drought conditions in many areas more often. This has affected the amount of drinking water available. Many that must rely on a well for water have seen it go dry due to a lack of rain. It's happening more often. That's something to keep in mind when shopping for a home.

If you have municipal water you may suffer also. In order to conserve water, many municipalities have changed their rates to punish people they feel are using too much. The county I lived in took water from a river to process into drinking water. Twice they asked for a waiver from the US so that they can take water from the river bottom, closer to the muck than is normally allowed. They also wanted to put more chlorine in the water than the standards allowed. They claimed the water was safe to drink, but it didn't look or smell like anything I wanted to drink.

Water or the lack of it is a serious issue in Florida. Up north I was billed for water quarterly, and considered the bill a nuisance because I had to write a check for such a small amount. When I moved into my first home in Florida, I cleaned everything inside and out, washed the car and topped off the pool. My first water bill for the month was over a hundred and fifty dollars. For a month! I called the water company to have the obviously incorrect bill straightened out. Instead, I was the one that got straightened out. Water was going to cost me much more and there wasn't anything I could do about it except conserve. If you live on a fixed income or on a tight budget, get the facts on the cost of water and sewer service for that area you are considering, before you sign the offer on a home.

Thirsty Lawns

If you buy a home that does not have a sprinkler system, your lawn will most likely die over time. It will also become brown and brittle during the winter because it almost never rains in most of Florida in the winter months.

If you have a sprinkler system you can keep your lawn green lawn, but you will have to cut it more often, or pay more to have someone do it. A sprinkler can also come with some unwanted responsibilities during droughts. Many municipalities will limit the use of your system to only certain times of specific days. They will also change those times and days and you had better keep up with their program or you could face a large fine.

Many homes with central water, have a well just for the sprinkler system. With this "yard well" the water is free. Wells are lot less expensive to put in than up north, because the water is closer to the surface. A sprinkler hooked up to the central water source will cost you a small fortune compared to one that is supplied by a yard well.

A drought in my area got so bad that you were only allowed you to water early in the morning, one day a week. They also gave every county employee the power to write tickets for fines if you didn't comply. Imagine a county janitor in the neighborhood that can slap you with a $500 fine over watering your yard.

Florida is the also lightning capital of the world. Blackouts, brownouts and power surges are common and can throw off the timer on your sprinkler system. That can make you a lawbreaker if you aren't there to catch it.

Boating is More Fun with Water

Have a boat or always wanted one? If you plan on buying a waterfront home with access to gulf or ocean, make sure you get all the facts on the depth of the water leading out. Waterfront property with access is highly desired by boaters and therefore some of the highest priced real estate available. You will not only pay much more to purchase it, but you will pay higher taxes every year than for the same exact home not located on water.

I have worked with many couples just moving down that have conflicting desires regarding a boat and waterfront homes. The issue is the huge difference in the type of home you can get for the same money, waterfront (with access to large water) compared to non-waterfront.

If you have $250,000, you may be able to get a large newer home with high ceilings, granite counter tops, heated spa that spills into a caged pool if it's not on a waterfront lot. For the same money, you may be able to get a well located waterfront lot with a small old shack that needs a total renovation. Usually it's clear to the wife, she wants the big comfortable new home. He wants the waterfront. Unless you have been avid boaters for years, she is right. You will be happier in the nicer home, based upon feedback from many of my home buyers that faced this same choice.

I not only sold newcomers waterfront homes but I lived on a canal and saw what happens. New buyers from up north that never owned a boat before buy a costly waterfront home and move in. They buy a boat. They use it every day, for the first couple of weeks. Then it's once or twice a month. After a year, the lonely boat just sits on the lift, unused and dropping in value. Finally, after just a few years just before it's completely worthless, they sell it. Do you know the two happiest days in a boater's life? The day he buys the boat and the day he sells it.

Did you know that Florida has experienced some of the worst drought conditions in its history recently?

Many waterfront properties have canals that lead to a creek or river on the way to the ocean or gulf. If you are a new boater, make sure you learn what kind of boat and draft you will likely have, before you spend the extra cash for waterfront. Many new residents pay a fortune for a waterfront home only to learn they can't get their new boat out to the big water because the canal is not deep enough two blocks away from their home. Or the boat you bought can't fit under the bridge between you and the Gulf.

Serious droughts in recent years meant lower water levels in normally boat-able waterways that have prevented the use of a boat. There are also waterways that are only passable during high tide or during the summer when the river and creek levels are higher from the rainy season.

If you are buying a waterfront home for boating, make sure you get a real estate agent who is a waterfront specialist. Make sure that isn't just something they put on their card, and don't even own a boat. Find an agent who lives on water themselves, has a boat, uses it regularly and loves boating. It won't cost you a penny to work with an expert like this, but the advice will be priceless. The best agent is the one that can show you homes by taking you there in their boat, right to the homes own dock. You can get free help in finding the right agent to work with from a service I run, listed in the back of this book.

Orange Glow and Smoke Smell at Night

You may have visited the state many times without

ever seeing or even hearing about a wildfire. In winter, it almost never rains. Because the sun is still very strong, it dries out all the brush and creates a fire hazard. A violent lightning storm can start numerous fires. Fire season starts about the same time hurricane season ends every year.

Just when you are safe from evacuations and hurricanes, a wildfire may cause one. These fires can burn for hours, days or weeks. In the area I lived in, you could count on at least one big wildfire every year. You'd see large clouds of smoke forming in the air, and smell and taste the smoke with every breath. When I first moved down, I drove towards the first one I saw. I ran into a police line blocking off the area. Lots of people were there to watch. I could see homes that were untouched by the fire but all the trees and brush of the vacant lots around them were charred to a crisp. Boats, sheds, anything near the vacant lots were burnt too.

There was a large state park preserve near my home that seemed to have fires every year. The fire department even started "controlled burns" to cut down on the amount of combustible brush. At night you could see the large red and yellow glow of the fire not that far away. You could smell the smoldering ashes for days afterward. This alone did not affect most homeowners to the point of moving, but was a contributing factor when a fire got so close that the firemen were hosing down their yard and home just as a precaution.

It is just something you should be aware of if you are going to be shopping for a new home. You may have trouble sleeping while smelling smoke and seeing the glow of a large fire in your window instead of the normal dark of night. These fires rarely make it into a neighborhood filled with homes, thanks to the fire crews. If you were close to buying in a certain neighborhood and wanted to know about the wildfire danger, I would contact the closest fire department rather than ask the real estate agent or owner.

Flooding

Shortly after I first moved to Florida, I experienced what was called a "no-name" storm. It started to rain one day and continued to rain for 5 days straight. It rained day and night without stopping. I had never seen anything like it before. My newer home sat up many feet higher than the road. There was also a grass greenbelt swale (man-made depression) behind my home that drained water away to canals that eventually led to the Gulf. Well, I watched as the water slowly started to fill the road and the swale, making my home an island. As the days went by the water slowly rose climbing toward my home. We were advised by the authorities to stay inside if it was dry or go to a shelter if your home was flooding. How you were supposed to get to the shelter, I didn't know. The water that filled the street was so high; I did not want to risk driving through it.

When the rain finally stopped and the water in the street went down to just a couple of inches, I went out for a drive in it. I drove around and my newer golf course community, and a nearby one where the homes were a little older. They were built before the newer building codes. These older homes were built right on ground that was the same level as the road. These people were already putting piles of carpet, furniture and other flood damaged belongings out for the trash man.

My home had been built to newer home elevation requirements. I didn't have any damage at all. The older homes were seriously flood damaged. That's why those older homes are costly to insure. Something to consider when shopping for a home here.

The strange thing about the "storm" was that there was no advance warning from the weather forecasters or anybody ahead of time. It was just supposed to be a few days of mostly rain that turned into heavy rain for five straight days. Afterword's I got a few calls from people who wanted to sell their flood damaged home and head back north.

Heavy down pours are a fact in Florida. Try to avoid older homes with poor elevation, especially if they are located in a designated higher risk flood zone. In these homes, even if you're lucky enough to avoid flooding, the high cost of flood insurance will get you.

Snakes Alligators Bugs

I'm going to mention these three separate issues as if they were pretty much the same. The state you are now living in probably has at least some of these creatures. Florida just has a lot more of them.

When I lived up north, I may have encountered a snake every couple of years. That includes jogging, biking and hiking on trails through the woods and mountains. If you move to Florida, your encounters with the slithering reptiles will increase, especially if you plan to experience parks, beaches and the outdoors often.

Snakes, like gators are more active when it's warmer. They also like to eat geckos, the non-English speaking kind that doesn't get a paycheck from Geiko. Geckos are abundant, fast, nervous lizard-like little creatures. The ones in Florida are too busy running for their lives to save you any money on car insurance. They are faster than the bugs they eat. When inside your pool cage, they can entice a snake to enter looking for a meal.

It's a Little Snaky Out Today

I once encountered five snakes in about 45 minutes while jogging along a bike trail one sunny summer afternoon. Four of them just slithered quickly across the trails macadam in front of me. There was one snake however, that was very thick and about 5 foot long with a rattle at the end that just stopped, laying almost end to end the width of the trail. So I stopped about 30 feet from it. I wasn't about to try to go around or over it. So I just waited. After a few minutes it slowly moved away and disappeared into the tall grass on the side if the trail. I finished my jog. Hope you aren't a snake hater.

Alligators Eat Pets and People?

You are more likely to encounter alligators in the
southern part of the state than the northern counties.
Do you have a little dog that is like part of the family?
Then you may want to consider the cooler northern
part for Fido's sake. Every time a small pet is eaten by
an alligator anywhere in the state, it makes the
headlines in Florida. Apparently gator eats pet stories
sell a lot of papers.

After living in the southern half of Florida for many
years I realized that any canal, lake, pond, large
puddle or drainage pipe could be home to an alligator,
if even for a short time. I have seen golfers on a green
near a lake putting calmly, not realizing that an eight
foot alligator is sunning himself just a short distance
away. While looking for my golf ball, I nearly walked
right up to what I thought was just a small log floating
near where my ball went. A golf buddy yelled, warning
me that it was a gator. Its body and most of its massive
head was hidden below the surface of the dark water.

Occasionally there will be reports of someone being
killed by an alligator. Just like pet deaths by gators,
these events are hyped by the media. Often the victim
was engaging in an activity that probably wasn't such a
great idea, like going for a swim in a lake that is known
to have alligators. For a few, just innocently taking an
evening stroll near water turned tragic.

Gators like to travel at night. I've read about people
waking up to find a gator in their pool. Reporters love
to cover stories like this. I did check my pool a little

more carefully before diving in after reading that.

Bugs Bugs Bugs

Do you know what a fire ant hill looks like? They are usually very small and hard to notice. That is until you encounter one the first time. Fire ants will swarm and start biting before you realize what is happening. Every bite stings and could last for hours. Learning how to spot these mini monsters can save you from a painful learning experience.

Termites are also more of a problem here than most other states. See the latter chapter on what to look for in a home to help minimize the risk. You will want to stay away from any home that is or will be an easy meal for hungry termites. Termites are just about everywhere in Florida. That's fine, they have their natural purpose. Just keep their home and your home separate and you'll be fine.

Mosquitoes Hope You like Them

If your lanai or pool isn't screened, you won't enjoy the outdoors as often as you should. This is especially true the farther south you go. Dusk and dawn can bring roaming swarms of mosquitoes, looking for a meal of blood. I never smashed a mosquito on my arm and saw blood until I moved to Florida. To survive living in this state, you learn how to avoid them.

In the spring and summer, make sure your car has good wipers and plenty of windshield fluid. Often you will have to use your wipers, not for rain but to clear "love-bugs" and other insects from your windshield. When driving in the summer (all six months of it) large juicy insects' splatting on your windshield and immediately being baked by the powerful summer sun, is routine. You'll get used to it. The car wash business is good in FL.

While the pests mentioned in this chapter rarely were the main cause for moving back, they were mentioned as a contributing cause. Are you especially bothered by any of these critters? Once here, you won't be able to ignore them because they'll live closer to you than the Smiths next door.

Florida Alligator fun facts

Florida alligators can grow to about 15 feet and weigh a half ton

An alligator can run faster than a man in short bursts

An alligator can swim faster than you can paddle a canoe

An alligator can kill and eat smaller prey in one bite

Alligators use a "death roll" to kill larger victims by taking them underwater and spinning violently.

Three women were killed in Florida by gators in separate attacks in a one week period in 2006.

Florida Snake Fun Facts

There are 44 species of snakes in Florida, 6 are

venomous.

"Pit-vipers" cause 99% of all snakebites in the US. All pit-vipers like rattlesnakes and water moccasins can be found in Florida.

Florida Bug Facts

There are so many kinds of bugs in Florida they haven't all been cataloged yet. Over 150 new arrivals now consider themselves Floridians since 1986 alone.

Giant cockroaches are very common in wooded areas, yards, lanais and homes. They have been called "palmetto bugs" in an attempt to make them seem less disgusting, but they don't live in or have any real connection to that common Florida plant.

Sky Rocketing Insurance Rates

Record Hurricane Activity in 2004 and 2005

The cost to insure a property in Florida wasn't always the problem it is today. Huge losses in property damage caused by record breaking hurricane activity in 2004 and 2005 caused insurance companies to seek continual rate hikes or leave the state altogether.

In 2004 I was notified by the company that insured my homes for 10 years that they were not going to renew my policy. The reason? They were not renewing or writing any new policies in Florida. They were not going to do business in the state any longer.

I thought, no big deal, I'll just get another company. I called my insurance agent and was told only two companies were writing new policies in my area. My home at 10 years old and so close to the Gulf of Mexico did not qualify for either one of them. What? The only choice I had was the insurer of last resort, Citizens Insurance. This is a company the State of Florida had set up. The new cost, 300% more than I was paying. Nice. Almost $5000 a year for homeowners and flood protection.

New Resident Shock

Most new buyers coming from other states are shocked when they attempt to secure homeowners. They call the company they had been with for decades; only to find out they don't insure homes in the state. Or they may have capped the number of policies in the state and will not write new insurance.

Before insurance companies can raise rates in Florida, they have to get approval from state regulators because these companies often have many thousands of homes insured. If they approve a massive rate hike it would create a financial hardship for large numbers of citizens, especially those on a fixed income. So the state turns the rate increase down. So the company then does not renew existing polices or write new policies or leaves the state altogether. It's a costly mess.

You Can't Get Insurance at All, It's The Law

Earlier in the book we talked about hurricane season. Buying a home in Florida during this time can present a problem almost all northerners are unaware of. Let's say you have closed on the sale of your home up north. You are now in Florida with everything you own in the moving truck. You are ready to close and move into your new home and start living your Florida dream. You get a call, and are told you can't close. Because there are now active hurricanes (even though they are still far away) have prevented the insurance company from allowing the policy you have arranged to take effect. No insurance, no mortgage, no sale. It could be days, weeks, nobody knows. Now what do you do? You're homeless with all your personal belongings in an expensive rental truck and nowhere to go with it.

Why did this happen? In the past, there were people who would not insure their homes in order to save money. When a hurricane would approach their area, these people would run out and get insurance real quick, only to cancel it once the threat had passed. This wasn't fair to the insurance company that could be on the hook for huge losses after collecting only one month's premium. It also wasn't fair to homeowners who would have to pay higher rates to help cover that type of person's loss. So the State of Florida passed a law that prevents new insurance from being issued in any area within a certain distance of a where a named storm may be heading.

During the busy hurricane seasons of 2004-2005, there were parts of the state that you could not get insurance for weeks at a time, because there was always one storm or another threatening. I often had buyers that were prevented from closing because of hurricanes. A retired couple that drove down here to close, had to stay in a hotel for 12 days until insurance was allowed to take effect. It cost them thousands more than they counted on for accommodations, meals, and the additional days for the moving van.

When considering the purchase a home in Florida, find out what it will cost to insure it before you sign an offer to purchase. The cost to insure your new property could be far higher than where you live now. If the home you want to buy will really cost you $400 a month to insure, rather than the $50 a month it would cost up north, can you still afford it?

The scary thing is that no one really knows how high rates will go in the future. Insurance companies have a pretty good idea of how many car accidents are likely to happen in Florida next year, so it's easy to determine what to charge for premiums. After the record number of hurricanes and damage in 2004 and 2005, how can they know what's going to happen this year or next year? How do you charge to insure against such unknown and potentially catastrophic losses?

The rising cost of homeowners and flood insurance in Florida has definitely caused people to leave the state. It has forced many who are on fixed incomes out of their homes. To protect yourself, always determine the total cost of ownership in Florida including insurance, taxes, water and sewer and maintenance.

Different mix than home

Native Floridians

After living in Florida for a while you realize that most people you meet here are not from the state originally. You can usually tell which folks were born and raised here in Florida. My guess is that showering and dentistry are recent to the state. Just kidding, not all native Floridians look like their parents were cousins. Again kidding. Many born Floridians provide general labor we need like cutting the lawn or working in restaurants. Real Floridians are some of the nicest people you will ever meet, if you meet them before they've had their tenth beer of the day which is hard to do unless you meet them early in the morning. Again, just.....OK let's move on.

More seniors in the Same Area Can Slow Things Down

Have you ever sat behind a car that didn't move when the light turned green? Ever had to wait because someone had their shopping cart in the middle of the aisle and didn't bother to move it when they saw you coming? How about being in a long line of cars in the no passing zone when the driver in front is going way below the speed limit? In much of Florida, all that and more can happen to you in one day, every day. You either adjust to it or go nuts.

Moving to FL with Young Children

If most of what you know of Florida comes from visiting the theme parks or popular beaches, you may be in for a shock when you actually move here. The majority of your neighbors may be in their sixties, seventies, and eighties. This new scene may take some time to adjust to.

If you have young children and move into a neighborhood with a high percentage of seniors (which can be hard to avoid), your kids may not be too happy. Your children may not have many friends they can play and socialize with. Your next door neighbor in his eighties and who has lived on the block years before you moved in may get very agitated when a baseball goes into his yard. Or when a child rides a bike on the street in front of his house for any length of time.

All I am pointing out here is that Florida has a higher percentage of older residents than most other states. In some subdivisions it can be extremely high. If you move your kids a thousand miles away from their friends, to one where there aren't many kids at all, you may have a problem you didn't count on. If they become miserable, at least they will have one thing in common with that neighbor we talked about earlier.

If You Are of Retirement Age

If you are retired, moving onto a street where the residents are of like age and mind may be exactly what will make you happy. Judging from the growth of 55 and older only communities, you would not be alone in wanting to avoid the problems that plagued Dennis the Menace's Mr. Wilson. There can be many other advantages than the absence of annoying little children (if that's how you feel) in those communities, such as maintenance free living where the lawn is cut shrubs taken care of by others. That will be covered in a latter chapter.

East is Fast West is Slow

There are distinct differences between most of the east coast of Florida when compared to the west coast. The differences are environmental as well as social. The water of the Atlantic Ocean on the east cost has bigger waves, frequent seaweed and can get deep quickly. On the west coast the Gulf of Mexico water is usually clearer or translucent blue, warmer, and gentler. The I-95 corridor on the east coast has a faster pace, more northeast city-like. Along most of I-75 on the west, life has a slower tempo like the suburbs or country areas of northern states. East or west, the pace of life in Florida is usually slower than what you will find in a comparably populated area up north.

The Florida Lifestyle

When you live in Florida you will hear a lot about the Florida lifestyle. Advertisers use the phrase when pushing goods and services. Put a pool in and enjoy the Florida lifestyle. Elaborate outdoor furniture that duplicates your living room will allow you to enjoy the weather and nature. It's about rest, relaxation and reducing stress. The merchandisers will tell you that you need to buy a lot of extra stuff to enjoy it, but that is not necessarily true.

Life in Florida does have a slower pace, even in the cities and on the east coast. The beach towns and keys are where life is most relaxed. When you wait outside a restaurant near the beach until 11:30 a.m. for it to open, when the sign clearly states it opens at eleven, you learn what "keys time" means. The closer to the water you are, especially on the west coast, keys and islands, the more approximate times are.

This different way of life is just what some people are looking for. Others come here thinking they want a slower more relaxed pace, but soon feel that eating dinner at four in the afternoon and seeing the streets deserted by nine is more like death.

Rarely has pace of life or population age mix ever been mentioned to me as the sole reason for leaving. Many times it was one of the things mentioned by those that wanted to leave. A test as recommended later will help you decide if the area you are thinking of will be a good match for you.

Save on Taxes

Real Estate Tax Homestead Savings

The Homestead Tax Protection Act provides unique tax benefits if you own a property in Florida that is your primary residence. The act was designed to prevent homeowners from being taxed out of their home due to rising property values. The law was originally enacted to help seniors on a fixed retirement income but now benefits all Florida residents regardless of age. If you purchase a principle residence you will not pay taxes on the first $50,000 of assessed value.

Homestead exemptions are determined by how the property is owned on the first day of January. In Florida, real estate taxes are paid in "arrears", so they are due at the end of the year. If you buy a home in June that already has the exemption, you benefit by paying lower taxes at the end of the year. If the property does not have the exemption, you will pay the full tax. To get the exemption, you must own the home by January first, and apply for the exemption by March first to get the homestead exemption for the end of that year.

You can't get the homestead exemption on any non-owner occupied investment, commercial, or vacation properties. If you buy a 2 unit and rent both units, you don't get an exemption. If you live in one unit and rent the other one out, you get the exemption if it is your principle residence.

If you buy commercial or income property and you

live on it as your primary residence, then you may be entitled to get the exemption. As always, verify before signing an offer. The exemption can provide substantial savings on real estate taxes over the years.

No Individual State Income Tax in Florida

Almost every state in the US forces you pay a tax on your income, in addition to what you pay to the IRS for federal tax. Most states take between three and ten percent. Some states offer a break to seniors or the disabled. Florida does not charge any citizen a tax on their individual income. Keeping more of your income is nice; not even having to prepare a state return is refreshing.

Thinking of maintaining two or more homes in different states? Consult a qualified professional because financially, it may be best to declare the place you have in Florida as your principle residence and use the other place as a vacation home. You could save lots of money on income taxes and get better protection of your assets. More on that advantage later.

A Benefit When Home Values Drop

Another good thing about Florida is the way they reassess the value of properties on a yearly basis. Every year the property appraisers adjust the value of all properties in the county according to a formula that measures if property has gone up or down in value. Almost all states will increase your assessment and tax as values rise, but will forget to lower your taxes when values go down. Florida has a better system.

During Florida's frequent housing busts, I was relieved to see the real estate taxes on my home go down substantially when the value did. The same did not happen when I owned a home up north. In fact, in areas where the prices dropped dramatically in that northern state, the still high property taxes were often the reason properties would not sell. Buyers would see a bargain price on a property, but couldn't afford to buy it because of the high real estate taxes based on an outdated high assessment.

Best Asset Protection State

What is Asset Protection

Asset protection can refer to a number of different subjects. What we are going to cover here is passive asset protection. All you have to do is move to Florida, become a resident and you will automatically enjoy all of these protections. Florida is in the top three states in the US for laws that protect its citizen's assets.

Unlimited Protection Your Home Equity

When you become a Florida resident homeowner, the equity in your home is protected from creditors regardless of how valuable your home is. For example, you move to Florida and buy a home for $250,000. You get a Florida driver's license and register your car in the state. You now consider yourself a resident of Florida and your home your principle residence. It is now almost impossible for any potential creditors to touch your equity in that home or attach a judgment to it.

After becoming a resident, let's say you happen upon some bad financial luck such as a credit card balance you can't pay, or you are involved in an automobile accident and get sued. Even if they get a judgment against you, they can't come after your home to pay for it. In Florida your qualifying principle residence is exempt, off limits. In many other states, the judgment would attach to your home and they could force the sale of your home to pay the debt.

This is an unlimited exemption that covers your qualifying principle residence. All of your equity is protected whether it is $5,000 or $500,000. Most other states provide little or no such protection.

Not All Properties Qualify

You may never need it but this protection will give you free added financial security so may want to make sure that the property you purchase will qualify. For a home to qualify in an incorporated municipality (city or town) the property must not be on more than a half-acre.

In rural areas outside the city limits, the exemption allows up to 160 acres. How can you tell if an area is an incorporated municipality? If it has its own governmental agencies like its own police force, mayor and other city services it probably is. We are talking about cities and towns, not counties.

I lived in a town that had its own name and zip code, but it was not an incorporated municipality. All services were provided by the county. The counties sheriff and deputies provided law enforcement. The 160 acre rule applied there.

Be sure to verify that any property you buy will qualify, before you sign anything. This is a very important protection to have, just in case.

100% Protection of Your IRA and Other Qualified Retirement Funds

You've worked hard. You made the sacrifices necessary to put money away in your 401(k), IRA or other retirement savings plan. The last thing you want is an overzealous litigation attorney to file a law suit because of an accident or other misfortune and take everything in your retirement accounts.

In most states, creditors can go after your retirement funds because there is little or no protection provided by state law. Some states open the entire amount to creditors. Others protect only the amount that is reasonably needed for support, allowing the creditor to take anything above that amount. What is "reasonably needed for support"? That is open to the discretion of the judge in the case. The possibility that your life savings could be taken from you may be a powerful reason to look at moving to a state that provides better protection of your retirement assets.

If you become a Florida resident, just like the homestead exemption for your home, your retirement funds will be exempt from attachment by creditors. This exemption is also unlimited which means your funds are protected whether the amount is a thousand or million. Talk about financial security, peace of mind and being able to sleep at night.

As with the Florida homestead protection there are guidelines that can affect this otherwise wonderful protection. Your retirement funds may have to be held by a "Florida only" financial institution, because only funds held in the state may be exempt. If you live in New York and move your assets to Florida after you have been sued, they may not be protected. If you are moving to Florida and you want to know what your protection rights are under the law, contact a Florida attorney for advice before you move. I have provided some attorney contact information in the resource section in the back of the book.

Life Insurance Cash Value and Proceeds Protected

Do you have a life insurance policy? Is there some cash value to the policy such as with a whole life or a universal policy? If so, the entire value of the policy could be out of the reach of creditors once you are a Florida resident. The proceeds of the life insurance policy are also exempt from creditors of the policy owner. This is another protection to keep in mind because many other states offer no such safety.

Annuities Protected Too

According to Investorpedia.com, an annuity is a financial product that can provide a steady income to its owners, usually for the entire life of the owner. There are many different types, but financial institutions such as insurance companies offer these to people who are interested in securing an additional steady income from money they have to invest. They are popular with those who are approaching, or already enjoying retirement.

Most other states allow creditors to take all of this income to satisfy claims. Here again, Florida residents are afforded rare 100% protection of this income against creditors.

Protection in Bankruptcy for Floridians

Florida's excellent financial protection of its citizens even extends to bankruptcy. The amount of property you can keep after filing for bankruptcy is very different from state to state. The state of Florida has opted out of the regular federal property and asset exemptions and allows its citizens to keep more than any other state, according to attorneys there.

One of the largest exemptions is your home. The Florida constitution allows you to keep all of the equity in your home, even if it is worth a million dollars. Any state that forces their citizens to use the regular federal bankruptcy exemptions may only be able to keep up to $22,000. Obviously, if you are moving to the state and are going to be purchasing a home with cash, this can be extremely important.

Bankruptcy laws went through a major revision in 2005. In order to use the unlimited protection for your home, you have to be a Florida Resident for 3.3 years first. However, your equity may be fully protected for those 3.3 years by the homestead protection that we talked about earlier, until you do file. Consult a Florida attorney for specifics.

Disclaimer Reminder

The general information provided here is to make you aware of possible benefits of becoming a Florida resident, but it is not professional or legal advice. To find out more about asset protection and how it may benefit you personally, contact a qualified Florida

Attorney or CPA who practice in this field. Some contact information can be found in the back of this book.

Florida Living Options

Sell All and Move to Florida Full Time

This is the riskiest move of all. Most of the folks that I had to sell for because they wanted to move back home, came from this group. You probably have a less than fifty percent chance of being happy with this type of move, long term. This can also be the most financially devastating and emotionally draining move, if you find you've made a mistake and have to move back.

To make this kind of a move, most will have to sell their current home. The likely cost of doing that will be thousands of dollars including real estate commission, transfer fees and other expenses. If you are selling in a poor market you may be losing a lot more than, rather than waiting for better conditions to sell.

Next, you will purchase a new home in Florida. Again, there will be thousands in closing cost, especially if you get a mortgage. You will be losing even more selling your belongings or packing and moving them to a faraway state.

What if, after you move, you find you can't stand the seemingly endless hot humid weather? What happens if you miss the family more than you thought you could? What if after 6 months of summer everything about Florida bothers you or your spouse, and now you make a decision to move back? Now you will have to sell and pay more closing. Pay the movers again and pay closing costs a fourth time to buy again up north.

Besides the mental toll all of this unsettling will take, there is another financial hit you may take. Selling your home in Florida for a lot less than you paid. Having to sell a home to move from a place you hate could easily put you on the roller coaster real estate market at the wrong time.

Buying the right home in the right area at the best possible price, regardless of the where the market is in the cycle, will help you a lot. Since you will probably not be a real estate expert in the area you are buying, you need to have one on your side. Make that an honest one that will put your needs before her own.

In a ten year period, I sold a builders model for somewhere between $69,900 and $239,900. I mean the same exact home with lot and everything, turn-key you just move in. The value did not just go up. It would go down, up, then down again. Some buyers who paid over $200,000 for this home when the market was OK, would have a hard time getting $100,00 three years later in one period. The prices dropped that much that fast. So is it possible to move to Florida, realize you made a mistake and lose a lot of money when you have to sell? Absolutely. Is planning two major moves in just a couple of years while losing a ton of money on a home something you can afford?

Before selling and moving to Florida full time, please read how to test this, in the next chapter. There are people who made this kind of move and have been happy with it long term. You may or may not turn out be one of them. With poor odds and the high cost if it doesn't work out, you may want to give serious consideration to the other options given here. Always test your first choice, as discussed in the next chapter, before making any final decisions.

Owning in Florida and Your Home State

In talking with thousands of people who have moved to Florida, the folks with a home in Florida and their home state are by far the happiest with their living decisions. They are still connected to the state where they have lots of family, friends, and the same home they have lived in a long time. This arrangement works out well and is one you should consider.

We'll call them "sixers" for the rest of this book because most of them spend about six months a year at each home. Many are retired couples. Retirement allows them the freedom to travel when and where they wish. I have also met many self-employed individuals who have figured out how to achieve freedom of movement while continuing to earn income, thanks mainly to the internet.

Many sixers start arriving in Florida mid-October. They come down here and enjoy the best weather Florida has to offer. It is warm and sunny with little or no rain or humidity. The snakes and gators are less active. Bugs are less of a factor, probably because many additional birds come here to escape the cold northern winter and eat the bugs. Best of all, there are no hurricanes and no evacuations.

After these joyful people have had their fun at the golf

courses, theme parks, and beaches, they go back about April 15th. Some follow a strict pattern, some don't. I know a retired couple that has a nice cabin in northern Michigan and a nice home here. They let the weather tell them when to go back and forth. When it starts to get too cold for their taste up north, they come to Florida. When the humidity starts to bother them as they play tennis or golf, they go back.

I know other Floridians that leave when hurricane season starts. They stay north through the summer and spend Thanksgiving and Christmas with the family. They head to Florida after New Year's Day. If you ever traveled I-95 heading south in the beginning of January, you no doubt noticed many more cars, boats and RV's heading south.

The reason the sixers are so happy is obvious to full time Floridians. The sixers enjoy the best Florida has to offer. They come down when the weather is warm with low humidity. It's sunny every day because it rarely rains this time of year. The nights are cool, good sleeping weather. You rarely will have to use the heat or AC. No daily stress from watching a hurricane slowly making its menacing advances toward you. The lines at the theme parks are shorter, and it's cooler. You can enjoy being outside all day without drowning in your own sweat. For the sixers Florida truly is just like travel brochures pictures.

While enjoying the best time of year in Florida, they also escaped the winter back home. They did not have to shovel snow. They did not suffer the depressing cold sunless days looking out at leafless trees. Then, as the weather in Florida starts to turn hot, humid and hurricane season approaches, the sixers head north. Arriving north they are greeted by the bloom of spring flowers and leaves shooting out of tree branches. The days are warm and nights cool. They are also back among familiar surroundings, family and friends.

The sixers don't suffer depression from feeling separated or isolated from old family and friends. They arrange to spend the holidays that are most important to them with the family. What the sixers have figured out is how to enjoy the best of back home and Florida, while also avoiding the drawbacks of each.

The first thing most of these happy contented sixers did was buy a home in Florida. They became Florida residents by getting a driver's license, registering their cars and using their new Florida address as their principle residence when filling out their Federal tax returns. They now enjoy all the asset protection benefits discussed in earlier chapters, and are free from paying state income tax.

How to Affordable Two Homes, Same as One

Some of these joyful people still have the home up north they've had for years. Others sold that big home up north and used the cash to buy two less expensive homes, a smaller one not far from the one they just sold, and their Florida Home. It may be more affordable than you think. Replace your $300,000 home with a $150,000 home up north, and in Florida. Make Florida your principle residence so you don't have to pay state income tax anymore. Spend winter in FL where you won't need to pay to heat or cool the home, while saving up north by keeping the thermostat just warm enough so the pipes don't freeze.

The Florida Home and Motor Home Option

Another excellent choice to consider is to get a motor home instead of owning a home up north. Then stay at a RV resort up north near your family to escape the worst of the Florida summer and hurricane season. Many do this for three or four months every year. Some find a resort they love and stay there year after year. Others use the RV and time to travel throughout the US visiting national monuments and other interesting places during the summer. I've met some that travel with the same other couples from Florida every year.

Travel back and forth from Florida and hurricane evacuations are less stressful because you always have a comfortable place to stay stocked with whatever you want.

What would make you happiest? Having a complete change of scenery every year is something these folks love. They never have to live where it is cold and damp or terribly hot and humid. How about you?

The Big Picture

The main goal here is to prevent you from making one of the biggest mistakes of your life. The other is to offer ways that may improve your life, that you never considered before. You wouldn't plan a permanent move to Florida if you knew you were going to hate it and just want to move back in a year, would you?

From talking to hundreds of sellers that wanted to leave, I found many new Floridians started to realize within the first year of their move, that it wasn't going to work. For others, even though it took longer to decide to move back, there were things that really started to disturb them within the first year of their move also. Those things later proved to be the major causes that forced them to leave.

For everyone planning to move here full time, I strongly recommend a test run in the area you are planning to move to, before making a permanent move. Full time Floridians have the greatest chance of finding that they miss their home, family and friends in their home state. They also find that traveling back for holidays all the time or spending them alone are both bad choices. That you can't take another six to nine months of a hot and humid Florida summers. The following test run suggestion is for you.

About Seasonal Rentals

Just about everywhere in Florida there are seasonal rentals. These homes are fully furnished and equipped with nearly everything you have in your home. You just bring your toothbrush, clothes and swimsuit. Seasonal rentals are generally rented by the week or month. You can rent everything from small two bedroom older cottages to million dollar condos right on the beach.

Most seasonal rentals are rented by "snowbirds", northerners who come down and rent for January through March to avoid the worst part of the winter, then return home. Most of these rentals get booked for this time of year, and they aren't cheap.

You may think that sounds like a great idea. Hey, you could plan a trip like that for a test right now. Let the Florida sun warm your bones while everybody back home is freezing and shoveling snow. You will also find out if the Florida lifestyle suits you. Is this what I am suggesting you do? ABSOLUTELY NOT.

If you make a decision to live in Florida as a full time resident based on being here during only the winter, you will be making a huge mistake. Winters in Florida are great! It's warm, not hot. The humidity level is much lower than the rest of the year. It doesn't rain here in the winter, just warm sunshine every day. No rain and no thunder storms. Did you know Florida is the lighting capitol of the world? Not even the weatherman will mention hurricanes because they aren't a threat in the winter months. You can golf, bike, hike, and do anything outdoors without risking death by heatstroke. Best of all there aren't any hurricanes or forced evacuations.

I don't know anyone who moved from the alligator state, because of the winter here. Sure, there are minor complaints. The traffic is much worst what with all the additional cars with out of state plates going half the speed limit, stopping in the middle of the street without warning to gawk at something and of course, driving straight for miles with a turn signal on.

The golf courses are crowded as are the beaches, restaurants and stores. If you like to eat your early-bird special dinner at three in the afternoon you can count on standing in a line just to get into any place that has average or better food. These are just minor inconveniences really, that are easily tolerated because of the glorious weather. Florida in the winter is likely everything you've dreamed about. That's why you may want to consider options other than full-time residency. We'll talk more about that later.

No, what you need to do is live in the area you are considering through at least a six month Florida summer. You need to experience the thrill of hurricane season. Maybe you will be lucky enough to be ordered from your home for an unknown amount of time. You need to experience the worst of full time Florida living. Tropical storms, wild fires, swarms of bugs, heat, humidity, alligators, snakes and watching a hurricane as big as the state itself approach. Can it really be all that bad? That's what you need to find out.

Test for Potential Full Time Florida Residents

Find a seasonal rental in the area that you would like to move to. While these fully furnished homes command top dollar during the winter, they can usually be easily rented at a huge discount the rest of the year because they often just sit vacant. Rent a home or condo similar to what you want to buy.

For the purposes of this very important test, you want to learn what it really would be like to have to live through a Florida summer. The summer is a major cause that chases newbies back home. This is when it is as hot as a desert but with the humidity of a swamp. This is when hurricanes threaten and you may be forced to compete with thousands of others for a spot on the road, gas and a place to stay and other necessities of life. This is when alligators, snakes and bugs are more active. What you need to do is live through the full six months of a Florida summer in the area of "paradise" you want to move to.

Rent for at least six months, anywhere from April 15th through October 15th at a minimum. A test period of a year would be great, if finances allow. If a shorter test is what you must do, just make sure it DOES NOT include the winter months from December through March.

If you are saying, hold on now, isn't this going to cost a lot of money? Trust me, this test will cost you pennies on the dollar compared to selling, buying, moving, selling, buying and moving again. Most importantly, it will save you the heartache and possible health problems that kind of stress can cause. If during this test run you discover full time Florida would be a mistake, it will be a little money well spent. If you find you can be happy here full time, you will learn things during the test that will help you make smarter decisions when you do buy and move.

Beginning the test April 15th will hopefully test another major reason for dissatisfaction. Missing your family and the get-togethers. You will be in Florida for Memorial Day, Fourth of July and Labor Day. If your family normally gets together for Picnics or other celebrations for these holidays, you will be forced to miss them, or go through the expense and hassle or frequent trips back home. Try putting up with airport security or the traffic on I-95 for multiple round trips in a three month period. Keep in mind that later in the year you have Thanksgiving, Christmas and New years in a two month period. That's why a one year test may be best if you can afford it.

You may be thinking, well maybe the family will come down to Florida to visit us for the Fourth of July. We can all go to the beach, or Disney and it will be great. Don't do it! This is supposed to be a test of what living in Florida long term will really be like. Ask anyone who has lived in Florida for years and they will tell you that the family will want to come down. They will come down on vacation and you will have a wonderful time, in the beginning. After the first couple of years, they won't visit anymore. The travel time, hassle and expense just to repeat the same vacation over and over will keep them from visiting. For the purposes of this test, don't let the family visit. If you want to see them, you do the traveling. That is what is going to be like, sooner or later. You need to test this to see what it is really like.

Sixers Test

Planning on buying in Florida, but also maintaining a home up north too? Congratulations! Chances are that not only will you be happy with that decision, but it may also help you stay healthier while you enjoy a longer life. The healthiest older people I ever met in Florida belonged to this group.

Since this choice will probably work long term, the purpose of your test should be to determine what area and type of property would be best. If the thought of condo living interests you, but you never lived in one longer than a week on vacation, now would be the time to test that out. Will it be a dream, nightmare or somewhere in between?

If you have vacationed in the same area for many years, have friends or family there and can't imagine buying anywhere else, no test may be needed. You buy there. However, if you are like the majority of people who have visited Florida often but stayed mostly in tourist areas that you can't picture yourself living in, a short test will be desirable.

Since you may be only trying to decide what area and what type of property, your first step is research. Use the resources in the back of the book and the internet to learn about places to help identify areas that appeal to you.

Try to narrow it down to the three areas that you think you would most like to live. Plan a three month trip, spending a full month in each of the areas. Try to stay in "seasonal rentals", fully furnished homes and condos, not hotels. Make sure they are in regular residential areas like where you are thinking of buying in. Spending a full month in a home or condo with regular Florida residents as neighbors will give you a better feel for the place than if you were surrounded by rowdy partying tourist on vacation.

Useful Tips on Buying

Condo or Single Family Home

You probably have a snapshot in your mind of what you want your new Florida life to look like. Let me give you some warnings about what happened to others when the dream met reality. It's somewhat natural to make plans based on the perceived benefits but not seek the negatives that can go along with a move until long after commitments have been made. Being able to weigh the pros and the cons before deciding, your odds of getting things right are much better.

The first dream we are going to dissect is the condo dream. You may have a dream of the day you sell your up north home with snow shovel and move to a condo in Florida and retire. While living in this condo everything will be taken care of for you. You won't have to cut the grass, trim bushes, and paint or fix anything outside anymore. Now that you are retired you can just lie leisurely in a hammock and watch someone else do the work. You want have a care in the world. Well not exactly.

While it may be true that you may not have to do any of the outside maintenance or repair, you will be paying for it in the monthly condo fee. This is over and above your mortgage payment (if any), taxes, and insurance. You could live in a single family home and pay to have someone else take care of those very same things for the same cost or maybe less. The difference is you will have more control of the cost and how things are done, in your own home.

In a home, you could have the lawn cut for you but chose to take care of the flowerbeds and minor trimming yourself. Many people find puttering around the yard at a leisurely pace very relaxing. They get satisfaction from having a manicured property that they had a hand in bringing about.

In your condo dream, you are lying in a hammock with a cool drink and maybe taking in an afternoon nap in the fresh air. That may not happen as you plan. First of all, you probably won't be allowed to put one up, against the condo rules. If the condo association provides them, which is rare (liability issues), there may only be two of them for the use of 600 residents. If you ever get to use them, your time may be very limited and they may be located in a noisy, overcrowded rec area. Reading that novel or taking a nap may not be possible.

Avoid a Condo Nightmare

If you have lived in your own single family home for the last couple of decades, moving to a condo may not be something you will ever adjust to. I have sold many condos for owners who only lived there a short time because in reality wasn't at all as they had pictured it. They felt they didn't have control over the property they owned.

In one case, a newly retired mid-west couple decided in less than a month that condo living was not for them. They couldn't believe they weren't allowed to put a flowerpot outside of their front door. They just paid a high price in cash for the unit and wanted to brighten it up a little. They said almost every day since they moved in, they were told of something else they weren't allowed to do. They didn't care how much money they might lose, they wanted to sell and sell now. They quickly realized they needed a home that they can do what they want, just like they have for most of their lives.

In another case I helped a widow get a great deal on a large condo on the beach. She wanted a condo so all the outdoor chores would be done for her. I found out later that she was looking forward to plenty of visits from her family. That's why she wanted a place that large.

The very first time one of those visits took place, the weaknesses in her plan showed. The grand-kids felt cooped up inside the condo and wanted to go outside and play. They went to the pool. They went back and forth to the beach. They left their sandy flip-flops and sneakers outside the front door. The widow saw nothing wrong in any of this. Her neighbors however, did. Numerous complaints were filed against her with the condo association. Too much noise. Can't leave personal items outside your front door. All children on the property must be accompanied by an adult at all times. That ruined what was supposed to the first of many memorable family visits for her. She called me to put the condo up for sale the day after her family went back home. She sold and moved back home.

Can You Back Out of a Sale

If you make an offer on a condo in the state of Florida,

you have a 3 day right of rescission that begins after you get the condo docs. This gives you time to learn of all of the rules, regulations and restrictions imposed on your use of the property. You have the right to back out of the contract if you don't like what you find, if you do so within the 3 days allowed. The problem is that the documents can be a hundred pages and very confusing. Most buyers don't find it very good reading. Often they never read the whole thing or don't completely understand exactly what they are signing up for.

If you are buying a condo for the first time make sure you read everything. Write down all of your questions. Make notes of everything you don't understand completely. You deserve to get correct answers to all of your questions and learn if they are restrictions that you will not be able to live with. I would get answers from the people at the condo association office, not the sellers. I would not ask the Realtor unless they were a resident of the condo complex and you trust them. I would also do this by email, so I would have the answers in writing.

If you enjoy the freedom of doing what you like, when you like with the property you own, you probably won't like condo living. If you have lived in a condo or apartment in a large city for most of your life, then it could be a good choice for you. If you are buying a vacation home or going to live as a sixer, a condo may work, but don't guess. Do the test.

Deed Restrictions

The State of Florida is filled with subdivisions and communities where the home you purchase may be subject to deed restrictions. Deed restrictions are limits and rules on what you can do with and to your property, in addition to the normal government restrictions you may be familiar with. Most of these communities have a gate you must enter through, a "gated community". They also have a homeowners association, similar to a condo association. Some they may look like just a regular area on a public street with no gates to enter.

Unlike a condo, you do not have a 3 day right to cancel an accepted offer if you don't like the deed restrictions. Make sure you find out if the home is in a deed restricted area before you sign an offer.

Almost all gated housing areas will have deed restrictions so they are easy to spot. There are many communities that have been built to have a Mediterranean look and feel about them. A deed restriction in one of these gated areas could be that all homes must have a tile roof. Maybe the tile roof must also be a certain color so all the homes are uniform and fit the desired look of the community.

Let's say you buy a home in in one of these areas. In a few years, you need a new roof. So you get estimates. You're told that you can have a nice new shingle roof put on for $15,000, but the red tile roof required by this community will set you back $40,000. This one deed restriction alone is going to cost you more, but you won't have a choice. You gave up that right when you bought the home.

Deed restrictions can be a very good thing. I lived in a non-gated, deed restricted area where you could put on any kind of roof you wanted, as long as it met the newest building codes. It had restrictions that I thought were great and some that I found ridiculous. One said you couldn't have your garage door open longer than an hour. The drafters of that restriction must have thought a community looks neater with the garage doors closed so you won't have to look at other people's garage junk. That restriction irked some of my neighbors.

The reasons areas have deed restrictions are to protect property values by keeping the community nice and neat. You may agree with some or all of the restrictions of an area. Other people don't like being told what they can and can't do with their own property.

A drive through a nearby community made me glad I had purchased my pool home in the deed restricted community I did. This other community had a few large beautiful homes with manicured lawns. Right next door were small maintenance neglected homes with rusted cars and other junk in the front yard. Freedom from restrictions can have a price.

Caged Pool, Yes or No

This is a difficult question to give advice on because it is really just personal choice. I can just tell you how others have struggled with this choice and you can decide what's best for you. First, above ground pools are not looked upon very highly in most of Florida. So when we talk about pools here, we are talking about in-ground pools. Above ground pools generally will not be allowed in deed restricted areas. Where they are allowed, they can be a liability. They can cause a home to sell slower and for a lower price.

If you are considering the southern two thirds of the state, we will also assume that we are talking about "caged" in ground pools. A caged pool is one that has a cool deck (patio floor) poured around it, with a large aluminum frame surrounding the entire pool area allowing it to be screened in. This screened cage keeps all the bad stuff like mosquitoes and leaves out of your pool area. It makes the entire pool area seem more like an extension of your interior of your home because of this physical barrier between the pool area and the outside world.

The pool cage in combination with the lanai (patio screened in with the same materials as the pool cage) provide you with a large bug free area to enjoy the outdoors. This space feels like interior living space, but outdoors. During the winter you may spend more time outside in this space during the day, than inside. Many people have "exterior living room" furniture, stereo systems and flat screen TV's set up out there. This is one reason you may not want such a large home in FL since you will be spending more time in the healthier outdoor air. This does not apply to the six months of a FL summer if you stay here year round.

This cage also allows you to keep the sliding glass doors to your home wide open when the weather is beautiful. Many Florida homes have multiple pocketing sliders. When you fully open these it's like removing a wall and opening your entire home to the outside.

Pools are taken much more seriously in Florida because you can often swim all year. You never close the pool. In areas where almost all of the pools are caged, avoid pools without a cage to protect your resale value.

Now Should You Buy a Home with a Pool

When I show homes to buyers in the six to nine months of a Florida summer and its ninety degrees with high humidity, almost everyone wants a pool home. When showing homes in the winter when it's seventy with low humidity, it isn't as important to them at that moment. When it's hot, buyers will pay more for the pool home. When it's cooler, saving $20,000 seems more important.

Some people who buy a place without a pool because it was cool when they were shopping for homes in the winter decide that they must have a pool during the following summer. Sometimes a pool can be added to the home they bought. Many times that won't work because the pool contractors can't get the large equipment needed in the backyard to put the pool in. So to get a pool, they have to sell and buy another home. This cost more to buy, sell and move than if they if they choose a pool home to start with.

If you and your family never swim, and never want to go in the water, well a decision is easy for you. If you are going to live in Florida twelve months out of the year, or you think you might like one, then that will probably be your best choice. If you will be living near the beach and think that will be a great pool substitute, think again. Overcrowding, lack of parking, excessive litter and beach closings due to contaminated water and more are a lot to put up with on an ongoing basis.

Home Size Does Matter

What size home should you buy or build? That depends upon how much time you plan on spending there. If this will be your only home, it should be large enough to be comfortable year round. The following are some tips that may help you whether you will be living in Florida full time or living the life of a sixer.

Florida homes are often described as a 3/2/2. This means it has: 3 bedrooms/2 baths/2 car garage.

You will probably be spending a larger portion of your time outdoors than you have in the past. With large screened lanai's and pool cages, many activities like eating breakfast and reading the morning paper or news on the laptop may be done outside more often.

You may grill dinner outside daily, rather than weekly or rarely up north. Since the screened outdoor areas will become more like "living area" many find they do not need as much inside living square footage as they had up north. Why pay more in real estate taxes just for the pleasure of paying more to cool and clean space you never use?

The most desirable home will have at least 3 bedrooms and two full baths. If there are just two in your family, this allows you to have a home office and a separate bedroom and bath set up to accommodate overnight guests. Many modern FL homes have a large master bedroom suite and two fairly small bedrooms.

A two car garage at a minimum is what most buyers' desire. Most Florida homes will not have a basement. Even if you only have one car, the other bay will come in handy for keeping bikes, lawn equipment and storage.

Starting in the late eighties to early nineties, most new homes were built with cathedral ceilings and open floor plans. These homes live larger than older homes. A 1250 sq. ft. 3/2/1 built in the 1970's with flat eight foot ceilings and a long hall leading to three bedrooms, may seem too small and cramped. A new home of that same size with cathedral ceilings and an open split floor plan will seem larger and more livable. A split floor plan is probably your best bet. These homes have the master bedroom suite on one side of the home with other two bedrooms all the way over on the other side. This is ideal for separating the kids, office and guests from your sleeping quarters.

A 1250 sq. ft. 3/2 with a newer floor plan will probably be the minimum that is comfortable for full time living for two people. A newer home of this size with higher ceilings and split plan with screened lanai and pool can be very livable, and a good economical choice for sixer retirement home.

I have helped buyers just moving to Florida buy big homes because that is what they wanted, only to resell it soon after because they found it was too large.

There was one couple who bought a good size 3/2/2 with a separate family room not far from where I lived. When a vacant lot near that home became available, they bought it and built a much larger home and moved there. After just a few months they realized they made a mistake by moving into such a large home. The taxes were too high. It cost a lot more to cool than their other home. It took too long to clean the bigger place. They left and moved back north. How much did all that moving cost? From Michigan to Florida, to another home in Florida, then back to Michigan.

Flood Zones

According to FEMA, The Federal Emergency Management Association, all homes are in a flood zone and anywhere it can rain, it can flood. What matters most is if you are in a low, medium or high risk flood zone. If you are in a high risk zone and get a mortgage, you will be required by the lender to get flood insurance in addition to homeowners insurance. If you are paying cash, you can't be forced to buy flood insurance, but in Florida it would probably be foolish not to carry it if you are in a higher risk zone. If a home is damaged by flooding, chances are regular homeowner insurance won't cover any of the damages.

Building codes in Florida have changed drastically in the last couple of decades in an attempt to minimize the damage done by hurricane force winds and flooding. The new codes make builders bring fill dirt in, or build stem wall foundations that raise the base elevation of the floor of the home many feet above the surrounding ground, in many areas. In the old days, a builder would just come out and pour a slab and start building.

In many areas along the coast you will see a newer home built right next to a much older home. Even though both homes may be ranches, you can see that the new home sits up much higher off the road than the older home. In fact, the older home's front door may seem to be almost the same level as the road, whereas the newer home's door is many feet higher. If you had a flash flood with a foot of water, you can see how the older home could be completely flooded but the newer home would not be affected at all.

This is why an older Florida home may cost less to buy, but may cost you a lot more to own because of the higher insurance cost. When getting insurance on a home in a higher risk flood zone, an insurance agent can't even give you a quote unless you can provide an elevation certificate that shows the homes base floor elevation. You can get an elevation cert from surveyors. The seller may already have one from when they bought or built. Have your Realtor ask for it, it could save you a little cash. Lower elevation means higher risk and higher cost of flood insurance.

Make sure you get the facts on the elevation and insurance cost of a home before you sign anything. You don't want to be contracted to buy an older home because you wanted to save money, only to find it will cost you $500 a month extra to just insure it. You would have been better off buying a newer larger home with lower insurance cost, because the total monthly cost would have been the same.

Market Price Warning

Florida seems to have an economy and real estate market that is unique among the states. Sometimes it's isolated from, or more affected by recessions felt by the rest of the US. The housing market is usually in a boom or bust cycle. As a Realtor selling homes for over 12 years there, I have seen $99,900 homes that were worth $200,000 4 years later. I have also seen brand new homes that were sold for $239,000, worth only $100,000 three years later.

If times are good, and you buy in Florida, you may be paying way too much. When the economy is great, home prices increase in most states. When a recession hits, home prices usually just stall in the north, but they almost always drop in Florida. Often the drop is fast and painful. Property in the north usually holds the gains made during good times, Florida homes values usually aren't so lucky. That's my assessment after selling for well over a decade in both the north and FL.

If you buy in Florida when times are good, and then decide you want to move back when the economy is not so good, you may find that the home you bought is worth $100,000 less than what you paid. This is a big hit if you paid cash but could be even worse if you took out a mortgage. What happens when you are absolutely miserable in Florida and want out, but you owe $200,000 on a house that's only worth $125,000? Do you sell and write a check at closing for $75,000 plus closing to get rid of it? Or do you continue to live in an area you hate for years, hoping the value will go back up? Do you rent it and become a landlord from a thousand miles away? What happens if the tenants stop paying, don't move, and trash your home while living there without paying? I have seen that happen a lot. Or do you just move and stop paying the mortgage and get foreclosed on. The bank may get a judgment against you for the difference and chase you with it for years.

Those are all terrible options of course. If you are young you could have time to recover from financial setbacks. If this would happen later in life you may never recover. Please know where we are in the economic cycle before buying in Florida. In general, the best time to buy there is during a recession or when the economy has been slow for a while. Why? Because although prices may have stopped increasing in your home town, they probably dropped terribly in FL. Seek expert local advice. The economy in FL could be completely different than what is happening nationally or where you live in the north.

Become Immune to Price Drops

If you will be a sixer, none of this may be something you should be concerned with. Chances are you will keep the place you buy in Florida for years, through many business cycles. If you aren't looking to sell, the economy and real estate market won't affect you. If you do decide to sell, you will be more likely be able to choose the best time, because you won't be as motivated as a full timer who wants to get out now.

If you will be a full timer, you also may be safe. If you have done your research, rented and tested living there and loved it, then you may be immune to the market also. You can buy a home in paradise regardless of market conditions and enjoy the Florida lifestyle. You can watch the economy soar and sink. It won't bother you at all, because you aren't selling. If you could live in Florida forever, but do decide to sell, you can pick to best time to sell because you are in no particular hurry. You know that if now is not a good time you can just wait a few years and it probably will be a great time to sell.

I hope that this book helps you make the best decision possible so have an enjoyable life. Please make use of competent professional advice when needed in connection to your move, especially regarding financial matters you may not be familiar with or when buying real estate in an area new to you. Please visit www.FloridaMoveGuide.com for updates and news on moving to Florida written after this book was published. Your suggestions and comments (good or otherwise) that may help improve the information that this book provides are welcomed. It will be regularly updated and republished. Thank You.

Helpful Resources

Asset Protection

Assetprotectionbook.com - Best website pertaining to the subject and you'll find their famous list of how the 50 states of the US rank. Definitely worth a look to compare the state you are now in to states you may be considering moving to.

Asset Protection Book - The book written by the attorneys from the website mentioned above. It's available from online booksellers like Amazon and through bookstores.

State of Florida Official Website

www.MyFlorida.com - This is the place to go to learn everything you could possibly need to know like how to get a driver's license, where to get your car registration and to check if your real estate agent is actually licensed and if she has any disciplinary actions doled out to her. I could have put some of this in the book, but why waste your time listing hundreds of locations for services if only one will actually be the best for you. If you decide to move to the sunshine state, this site will help you become a citizen in good standing because you will learn how soon after your arrival you have to register your cars, get a driver's license, etc.

Homes/Real estate/Realtors

FloridaMoveGuide.com - Find a link to a free Realtor Referral Service endorsed by the author. Get a Realtor hand-picked especially to meet your real estate needs to sell up north and/or to buy in Florida or anywhere else.

Hurricanes

www.nhc.noaa.gov - The National Hurricane Center - The go to site for information of all kinds on hurricanes from preparing a hurricane kit to live tracking and predicted paths of and impacts of live hurricanes. This is the site that I checked on a regular basis when hurricanes were heading toward Florida because I could get updated information before it was available from news sources such as TV. This is where the TV meteorologist get their information from.

Research How to Find Areas to Move To

www.City-Data.com Researching Specific Cities/Towns in Florida and Nationwide - This is a MUST SEE site to do your due diligence BEFORE you decide to move to any particular city or town. Everything you could ever want to know about what kind of people live in an area including age groups, how many with college degrees, employment, etc. and more. They list churches, radio stations, everything. I learned things from this site about an area I lived in for 30 years but didn't know. A true, free with no sign up required, research treasure.

http://money.cnn.com/magazines/moneymag/ For what it's worth, this is one of the most publicized "where to move to" guides. Some years I agree with their selections and other years they name places I wouldn't even drive through to get somewhere else. I guess that means I won't get a great book review from them.

www.bestplaces.net

www.findyourspot.comhttp://money.usnews.com/mo ney/personal-finance

Alphabetical Index

Made in the USA
San Bernardino, CA
15 November 2012